THE ULTIMATE MEDITERRANEAN DIET COOKBOOK FOR BEGINNERS

Easy, Delicious, and Nutritious Recipes for Healthy Living Every Day \ Comprehensive 30-Day Meal Plan for Weight Loss and Wellness

Alger Baxter's The Ultimate Mediterranean Diet Cookbook for Beginners is a comprehensive guide to adopting the Mediterranean lifestyle with simple, delicious, and healthful dishes. Designed for novices, health-conscious individuals, and those aiming to lose weight, this cookbook features a precise 30-day meal plan to facilitate a smooth transition to healthier eating habits. The book addresses common issues with clear instructions, practical tips, and specific cooking times for each recipe, making it an invaluable resource for daily healthy living.

Who is the Author?

Alger Baxter is the author of this book and an authority in the culinary world. He has a doctorate and has been cooking for over two decades. His experience and knowledge make him the perfect person to show you the ins and outs of Mediterranean cuisine, the Mediterranean diet, and all its benefits for your health. After spending over 20 years perfecting his skills in the kitchen, the author has a good understanding of the challenges home cooks often face and has developed some practical solutions to help overcome them. His hands-on cooking experience and academic background make the tips and techniques in this book reliable and effective. The author's journey from passionate home cook to professional chef has given him the know-how to help you get your desired results. He's been on this journey himself, trying out different flavors, perfecting techniques, and figuring out how to create dishes that are not only really tasty but also bring joy and harmony to the cooking process. This book results from the author's experience and knowledge of cooking and philosophy. He believes cooking is about more than just the food. It's about creating a meditative and harmonious experience that nourishes body and soul. He aims to share this perspective with you and help you turn the cooking routine into a fulfilling and enjoyable practice. By following the guidelines in this book, you'll benefit from the author's extensive experience and practical advice, ensuring that you can create dishes that will impress and delight your family and friends.

Introduction

- **Are you ready to embark on a journey to vibrant health and delicious dining?**
- If you've ever found yourself craving a healthier lifestyle but struggled with where to begin, you're not alone. Many individuals face the challenge of navigating diets that promise results but lack practicality or flavor. In The Ultimate Mediterranean Diet Cookbook for Beginners 2024, you will discover a comprehensive solution to these common challenges.
- **Within these pages,** you'll find easy-to-follow recipes crafted specifically for beginners to the Mediterranean diet. Each recipe comes with practical prescriptions that fit seamlessly into your daily life, making healthy eating a sustainable habit rather than a daunting task. Imagine effortlessly preparing meals that not only support weight management but also enhance your overall well-being.
- **Authored by Alger Baxter**, a seasoned culinary expert with a passion for Mediterranean cuisine, this book combines traditional flavors with modern nutritional science. With Alger's guidance, you'll not only learn how to cook nutritious meals but also understand the profound impact that food can have on your health and happiness.

Copyright Disclaimer

Table of Contents

Table of Contents

Table of Contents

Table of Contents

BREAKFAST
RECIPES

Honey Oat Bread

 serves: 2

 Time: 30 mins

Cook Time: 10 mins

Ingredients

- 2 cups entire wheat flour
- • 1 cup oats (rolled or fast oats)
- • 1 tablespoon dynamic dry yeast
- • 1 1/4 cups warm water
- • 2 tablespoons honey
- • 2 tablespoons olive oil
- • 1 teaspoon salt

Directions

1. Start by dissolving the yeast in warm water in a large bowl and let it sit for 5-10 minutes until it becomes foamy. 2. Next, mix in the honey and olive oil. 3. Then, add the whole wheat flour, oats, and salt, and mix until a dough forms. 4. Knead the dough on a floured surface for 5-7 minutes until it becomes smooth. 5. Place the dough in a greased bowl, cover it with a clean kitchen towel, and let it rise in a warm spot for about 1 hour. 6. After the dough has risen, punch it down and shape it into a loaf. 7. Place the loaf in a greased bread pan and let it rise again for 30-45 minutes. 8. Preheat the oven to 375°F (190°C) and then bake the bread for 30-35 minutes until it is golden brown and sounds hollow when tapped on the bottom.

Avocado Toast with Poached Egg

 serves: 2

 Time: 20 mins

Cook Time: 10 mins

Ingredients

- 2 slices whole grain bread, toasted
- 1 ripe avocado
- 2 eggs
- Salt and pepper to taste
- Red pepper flakes (optional)
- Fresh herbs (such as parsley or cilantro) for garnish

Directions

Toast the slices of whole grain bread. While the bread is toasting, prepare the avocado by mashing it in a bowl with a fork. Season with salt, pepper, and red pepper flakes if using. Poach the eggs: Bring a pot of water to a gentle simmer. Crack each egg into a small bowl or ramekin. Create a gentle whirlpool in the water and carefully slide the eggs into the center. Cook for about 3-4 minutes for a runny yolk or longer for a firmer yolk.

Spread mashed avocado onto the toasted bread slices. Carefully place a poached egg on top of each slice. Sprinkle with salt, pepper, and fresh herbs for garnish. Serve immediately while the egg yolk is still runny if preferred.

Whole Wheat Pancakes with Greek Yogurt and Fresh Fruit

 serves: 2   Time: 15 mins   Cook Time: 6 mins

Ingredients

For the Pancakes:

- 1 cup whole wheat flour
- 1/2 cup finely ground almond flour (adds a nice texture and nutty flavor)
- 2 tbsp ground flaxseed (for omega-3 fatty acids and a touch of nuttiness)
- 1 tbsp honey or maple syrup (as a natural sweetener)
- 1 tsp baking powder
- 1/2 tsp baking soda
- 1/4 tsp sea salt
- 1 cup almond milk (or other plant-based milk)
- 2 large eggs
- 2 tbsp extra virgin olive oil (for a hint of Mediterranean flavor and healthy fat)
- 1 tsp vanilla extract
- 1/2 cup finely chopped fresh figs or dates (optional, for added sweetness and texture)

For the Topping:

- 1 cup Greek yogurt (plain, full-fat or low-fat)
- 1 tbsp honey (optional, for drizzling)
- Fresh fruit (such as berries, sliced peaches, or pomegranate seeds)
- A sprinkle of chopped nuts (such as walnuts or almonds)
- A pinch of ground cinnamon (for a warm spice note)

Directions

Prepare the Batter:

- In a large bowl, whisk together the whole wheat flour, almond flour, ground flaxseed, baking powder, baking soda, and sea salt.
- In another bowl, whisk together the almond milk, eggs, olive oil, honey (or maple syrup), and vanilla extract.
- Gradually add the wet ingredients to the dry ingredients, stirring until just combined. If using, fold in the finely chopped figs or dates.

Cook the Pancakes:

- Heat a non-stick skillet or griddle over medium heat and lightly grease with a bit of olive oil or cooking spray.
- Pour about 1/4 cup of batter onto the skillet for each pancake. Cook until bubbles form on the surface and the edges look set, about 2-3 minutes. Flip and cook until golden brown on the other side, about 1-2 more minutes.
- Keep pancakes warm in a low oven (about 200°F) while you cook the remaining batter.

Assemble and Serve:

- Stack the pancakes on serving plates.
- Spoon a generous dollop of Greek yogurt on top of each stack.
- Drizzle with a little honey, if desired.
- Garnish with fresh fruit, a sprinkle of chopped nuts, and a pinch of ground cinnamon.

Scrambled Eggs with Spinach and Olive Oil

serves: 2 ⏳ **Time: 15 mins** 🕐 **Cook Time:** 0 mins

Ingredients

- 3 large eggs
- Baby spinach
- 3 oz. Olive oil
- ½ tbsp Skim milk
- 1 ½ tbsp Salt
- 1/16 tsp or to taste
- Black pepper
- 1/16 tsp or to flavour

Directions

Pour the oil into a dish and heat over medium-high heat.
Place the eggs on a plate and beat them. Combine skim milk, salt, and pepper.
Fill the dish and stir occasionally.
When the mixture begins to coagulate, add the spinach and continue to heat until wilted.

Greek Yogurt Parfait with Nuts and Maple Syrup

serves: 2 ⏳ **Time: 30 mins** 🕐 **Cook Time:** 20 mins

Ingredients

- Granola, ⅓ cup
- Greek yogurt, ⅓ cup
- Almonds, 1 tbsp, chopped
- Cashews, 1 tbsp, chopped
- Berries, ½ cup, assorted
- Maple syrup, 1 tbsp

Directions

Pour a layer of yogurt into the glass.
Apply a muesli layer.
Add a third layer of almonds, cherries, and nectar.
Continue to use this framework until you've used it all.

Overnight Oats with Chia Seeds and Fresh Fruits

 serves: 2   Time: 40 mins   Cook Time: 20 mins

Ingredients

- Rolled oats , ½ cup
- ½ cup Chia seeds
- 2 tbsp Blueberries
- 2 tbsp Blackberries
- 2 tbsp Almond milk
- ½ cup Water
- ¼ cup Banana
- Gound cinnamonptional)

Directions

Choose an airtight container. Add berries if desired. Blend well. Chill for 8 hours.
In the morning, add the fruit and relish.

Blueberry-Oatmeal Cakes

 serves: 2   Time: 30 mins   Cook Time: 5mins

Ingredients

- 2 ½ cups old-fashioned rolled oats
- 1 ½ cups low-fat milk
- 1 huge egg, softly beaten
- ⅓ cup pure maple syrup
- 2 tablespoons canola oil
- 1 teaspoon vanilla extract
- 1 teaspoon ground cinnamon
- 1 teaspoon baking powder
- ¼ teaspoon salt
- ¾ cup blueberries, fresh or frozen

Directions

In a massive mixing bowl, consolidate the oats and milk. Cover and refrigerate for approximately 8 hours, but up to 12 hours, until the majority of the liquid has been held.
Preheat the grill to 375° Fahrenheit. A cooking sprinkle cooking seasoning over a 12-cup nonstick bread roll skillet.
Mix the oats with the egg, maple syrup, oil, vanilla, cinnamon, baking powder, and salt until thoroughly combined. Divide the hitter among the bread roll cups (approximately 1/4 cup each). Top each with 1 tablespoon blueberries.
Heat the oat cakes for 25-30 minutes, or until they quickly return when contacted. Allow it to cool in the fridge for ten minutes. A paring edge could be used to unravel and kill. Serve warm.

Spinach and Feta Wrap

 serves: 2    Time: 30 mins   Cook Time: 10 mins

Ingredients

- 2 large eggs
- 1 cup fresh spinach leaves
- 2 tablespoons crumbled feta cheese
- 1 whole wheat tortilla or wrap
- Salt and pepper to taste
- Olive oil or cooking spray

Directions

In a bowl, whisk the eggs and season with salt and pepper. Heat a holder over medium heat and lightly coat with olive oil or cooking sprinkles.

Add the fresh spinach to the meal and sauté until wilted. Place the beaten eggs in the container with the spinach. Sprinkle the eggs with crumbled feta cheddar. Cook, mixing occasionally, until the eggs are well cooked.

Warm the whole wheat tortilla in the microwave for a few minutes as required. Place the broiled egg, spinach, and feta mixture at the tortilla's point of confluence. Overlay the sides of the tortilla and wrap it up tightly, obtaining the items. Serve immediately.

 Breakfast Salad with Egg & Salsa Verde Vinaigrette

 serves: 2   Time: 20 mins   Cook Time: 10 mins

Ingredients

- 3 tablespoons salsa verde, such as Frontera brand
- 1 tablespoon + 1 tsp. extra-virgin olive oil, divided 2 tablespoons chopped cilantro, plus more for garnish
- 2 cups mesclun or other salad greens
- 8 blue corn tortilla chips, broken into large pieces
- ½ cup canned red kidney beans, washed ¼ avocado, sliced 1 large egg

Directions

In a small mixing dish, add the salsa, 1 tablespoon of oil, and cilantro. In a shallow dinner plate, combine half the mixture with mesclun (or other greens).

Top the salad with chips, beans, and avocado.

In a small nonstick skillet, heat the remaining 1 tsp of oil over medium-high heat. Fry the egg until the white is fully cooked but the yolk is still pretty runny, which should take around 2 minutes.

Serve the egg over the salad. Drizzle with the remaining salsa vinaigrette and, if wanted, garnish with additional cilantro.

15

Almond Flour Pancakes with Sugar-Free Syrup

 serves: 2   Time: 10 mins   Cook Time: 5 mins

Ingredients

- 1 cup almond flour
- 2 large eggs
- 1/4 cup unsweetened almond milk (or any milk of your choice)
- 1 tablespoon olive oil or melted butter
- 1 tablespoon erythritol (or any sugar substitute of your choice)
- 1 teaspoon baking powder
- 1/2 teaspoon vanilla extract
- Pinch of salt
- Sugar-free syrup, for serving

Directions

In a mixing bowl, whisk together almond flour, eggs, almond milk, olive oil or broken spread, erythritol, baking powder, vanilla concentrate, and a sprinkle of salt until thoroughly blended.
Allow 5-10 minutes for the almond flour to absorb the liquid and thicken.

Heat a nonstick skillet or griddle over medium heat and gently coat with cooking seasoning or a small amount of olive oil.
Pour 1/4 cup hotcake batter onto the griddle for each pancake.
Cook the pancakes for 2-3 minutes on one side, or until bubbles form in a shallow area and the edges seem solid.
Flip the pancakes and cook for a further 1-2 minutes on the opposite side.

Quinoa Porridge with Cinnamon and Apples

 serves: 2   Time: 20 mins   Cook Time: 5 mins

Ingredients

- 1/4 cup quinoa, rinsed
- 3/4 cup unsweetened almond milk
- 1/2 teaspoon ground cinnamon
- 1 small apple, diced
- 1 tablespoon chopped walnuts (optional)
- 1 tablespoon unsweetened shredded coconut (optional)
- Stevia or erythritol to taste (optional)

Directions

Mix quinoa and almond milk in a small skillet. Intensity will eventually result in bubbling; then, reduce power to low and simmer for 15-20 minutes, or until the quinoa is cooked and the mix has thickened.
Add the ground cinnamon and chopped apple. Cook for another 2-3 minutes, or until the apple feels tender.
Disconnect from the power and let the porridge cool somewhat.
Blend in chopped walnuts, shredded coconut, and your preferred sugar.
Serve warm and enjoy your low-carb quinoa porridge with cinnamon and apples!

Egg Muffins

 serves: 2   Time: 40 mins   Cook Time: 20 mins

Ingredients

- 6 eggs
- 1/4 cup milk
- 1 cup diced vegetables (bell peppers, spinach, tomatoes, onions, etc.)
- 1/2 cup shredded cheese
- Salt and pepper to taste

Directions

Preheat the oven to 350°F (175°C). Grease a roll tray or use silicone roll cups. In a mixing dish, combine eggs, milk, salt, and pepper.

Distribute the chopped veggies and shredded cheddar evenly among the bread roll cups. Pour the egg mixture over the veggies and cheddar, filling each cup almost to the top.

Cook for 20-25 minutes, or until the egg has set and the tops are perfect. Allow them to cool to some extent before removing them from the rolling tin.

Zucchini Bread Oatmeal Bowl

 serves: 2   Time: 10 mins   Cook Time: 5 mins

Ingredients

- 1/2 cup rolled oats
- 1 cup almond milk (or any milk of your choice)
- 1/2 teaspoon ground cinnamon
- 1/4 teaspoon ground nutmeg
- 1/2 cup grated zucchini
- 1 tablespoon honey or maple syrup
- Chopped nuts or raisins for topping (optional)

Directions

Combine moved oats, almond milk, ground cinnamon, and ground nutmeg in a pan. Mix in the ground zucchini and simmer on medium heat, mixing occasionally, until the oats are cooked and the mixture thickens.

Add honey or maple syrup to taste. Before serving, top with chopped nuts or raisins as needed.

 # Banana Chocolate Chip Pancakes

serves: 2   Time: 10mins   Cook Time: 0 mins

Ingredients

- 1 ripe banana, mashed
- 1/4 cup almond flour
- 2 tablespoons coconut flour
- 1/4 cup unsweetened almond milk
- 1 tablespoon unsweetened cocoa powder
- 1 tablespoon sugar-free chocolate chips
- 1/2 teaspoon baking powder
- Pinch of salt
- Coconut oil for cooking

Directions

In a mixing dish, combine crushed banana, almond flour, coconut flour, almond milk, cocoa powder, sugar-free chocolate chips, baking powder, and a pinch of salt. Blend until smooth. Heat coconut oil in a nonstick pan over medium heat.

Spoon the hotcake batter onto the griddle, forming small flapjacks. Cook for 2-3 minutes per side, or until well browned.

Rehash with the remaining batter. Serve heated with no sugar syrup whenever desired.

Egg White Frittata

 serves: 2   Time: 20 mins   Cook Time: 5 mins

Ingredients

- 8 egg whites
- 1 tablespoon olive oil
- 1 small onion, finely chopped
- 1 bell pepper (red or yellow), diced
- 1 cup cherry tomatoes, halved
- 1 cup baby spinach
- 1/2 cup black olives, pitted and sliced
- 1/4 cup crumbled feta cheese
- 2 tablespoons fresh basil, chopped
- 2 tablespoons fresh oregano, chopped (or 1 tablespoon dried oregano)
- Salt and freshly ground black pepper, to taste

Directions

Preheat Oven: Heat oven to 375°F (190°C).

Sauté Vegetables: In an oven-safe skillet, heat olive oil over medium heat. Cook onion and bell pepper until tender, about 5-7 minutes. Add cherry tomatoes and spinach, cooking until spinach is wilted.

Prepare Egg Whites: Whisk egg whites in a bowl. Pour over vegetables in the skillet. Season with salt and pepper. Cook for 2-3 minutes on stovetop.

Add Toppings: Sprinkle olives and feta over the egg whites. Bake: Transfer skillet to oven and bake for 10-15 minutes, until set and golden.3 minutes before serving, add the yolks for color.

Cool & Serve: Let cool slightly, then slice and garnish with fresh basil. Enjoy warm or at room temperature!

18

Spinach and Tomato Quesadilla

serves: 2   Time: 30 mins   Cook Time: 5mins

Ingredients

- 2 low-carb tortillas
- 1/2 cup shredded vegan cheese
- 1/2 cup baby spinach leaves
- 1/4 cup diced tomatoes
- 1/4 cup diced red onion
- 1/4 teaspoon garlic powder
- 1/4 teaspoon onion powder
- Salt and pepper to taste
- Olive oil for cooking

Directions

Heat olive oil in a pan over medium heat.

Place one tortilla in the griddle, then evenly distribute half of the obliterated vegetable darling cheddar.

Over the cheddar, arrange the youngster spinach leaves, chopped tomatoes, and diced red onion.

Season with garlic powder, onion powder, salt, and pepper.

Top with the excess obliterated vegetable darling cheddar and place the tortilla on top.

Cook for 2-3 minutes per side, or until the tortillas are golden brown and the cheese has crumbled.

Remove the skillet from the heat and allow to cool before cutting into wedges.

Serve hot and indulge in your low-carb spinach and tomato quesadillas!

Sweet Potato Bisque

8 Servings

INGREDIENTS:

- 2 pounds (908 g) orange
- sweet potatoes
- 2 carrots (about 7 ounces [196 g])
- 1 parsnip (about 5 ounces [140 g])
- 1 onion (about 5 ounces [140 g])
- 1 quart + 1 cup (1 L + 235 ml) chicken Bone Broth
- 3/4 cup (180 ml) full-fat coconut milk Sea salt to taste

 1 hr 5 mints

 5/10

Preparation Steps:

Cut the yams, carrots, and parsnips into strips and serve. Cut off the onion. Combine the veggies and chicken stock in a stockpot.

Cover and power as a result of rising overcentered energy, then reduce the power to medium and simmer until the veggies are tender, about 20 minutes.

Remove off the power and combine with a submersion blender until smooth.

Stir in the coconut milk and season to taste with salt. Separate the soup into 5 sections or glass containers.

cook

Sweet And Sour Asian Cod With Rainbow Slaw

2-5

INGREDIENTS:

- 4 servings 4 (6-ounce [168 g]) cod fish fillets
- 1 tablespoon (15 g) coconut oil
- 1/4 teaspoon ginger powder
- Sea salt to taste

FOR THE SWEET AND SOUR ASIAN DRESSING:

- 3 tablespoons (45 ml) coconut aminos
- 2 tablespoons (30 ml) avocado oil
- 1 tablespoon (20 g) honey
- Juice of 1 lime
- 1/2 teaspoon ginger powder

Cooking

FOR THE RAINBOW SLAW:
1/4 purple cabbage (about 1/2 pound [227 g])
1 baby bok choy (about 5 ounces [140 g])
2 carrots (about 5 ounces [140 g])
4 radishes (about 4 ounces [112 g])
3 scallions

45 mints

Preparation Steps:

- Clean the fish with paper towels. In a large skillet, condense the coconut oil over medium heat. Combine the cod filets, ginger powder, and salt to taste. Cover and cook for 4 minutes per side, or until the salmon is flaky. (The cooking time of the fish may vary depending on its thickness.) Transfer to a plate to cool.
- Prepare the slaw by cutting the cabbage, bok choy, carrots, radishes, and scallions carefully. Place in a large mixing basin and combine thoroughly.
- Make the dressing by combining the coconut aminos, avocado oil, honey, lime juice, ginger, and garlic powder in a bowl. Combine well and chill until needed.

4/10

Tostones

Ingredients:

- 3 green plantains
- 1/3 cup (80 ml) avocado oil or tallow

5-servings

Preparation Steps:

Wipe the tops and bottoms of the plantains and peel with a vegetable peeler. Cut the peeled plantains into 1" (2.5cm) thick slices.

In a large frying pan, heat the avocado oil over a medium heat. When hot, add the plantain slices in a single layer (do not cover). Repeat for three minutes on each side. You may need to do this two or three times.

Use an open spatula to transfer the cooked plantain to a dish lined with paper towels. After cooling, place the plantain between two pieces of tissue paper and secure with the flat back of a measuring cup to make it 1/4 inch (6 mm) thick.

cooking

2 hours

Sweet Potato Hash

serves: 2   Time: 20 mins   Cook Time: 5 mins

Ingredients

- 2 medium sweet potatoes, peeled and diced
- 1 onion, diced
- 1 red bell pepper, diced
- 2 cloves garlic, minced
- 2 tablespoons olive oil
- Salt and pepper to taste
- Optional: paprika, cumin, or other preferred spices

Directions

Heat olive oil in a skillet over medium heat. Add diced sweet potatoes to the skillet and cook for about 5-7 minutes, stirring occasionally, until they start to soften.

Add diced onion, red bell pepper, and minced garlic to the skillet with the sweet potatoes.

Continue cooking for another 5-7 minutes or until the vegetables are tender and slightly caramelized, stirring occasionally.

Season with salt, pepper, and any preferred spices like paprika or cumin. Stir to combine.

Once everything is cooked through and nicely browned, remove from heat. Serve the sweet potato hash as a side dish or as a base for fried or poached eggs.

Loco Moco Burger

3-4   50 mint   cooking

Ingredients:

For the cauliflower rice:
- 0.5 head of cauliflower
- 1 Tablespoon of coconut oil
- Salt to taste

For the Loco Moco:
- 0.5 lb of ground beef (225 g)
- 1 Tablespoon of onion powder (7 g)
- 1 Tablespoon of garlic powder (10 g)
- Sea salt, to taste
- 2 Tablespoons (30 ml) coconut oil
- 1 onion (110 ml), peeled and sliced
- 15 white button mushrooms (150 g)
- 2 cloves garlic, peeled and sliced
- 2 Tablespoons (16 g) arrowroot powder
- 1 cup (240 ml) beef broth
- 1/2 large avocado (100 g), sliced
- 3 oz pickled beetroot, diced small (80 g) or 1 small beet boiled and peeled
- 2 Tablespoons (2 g) parsley, to garnish

Preparation Steps:

After smashing the cauliflower florets, pour them on a plate with the coconut oil and fry for 8-12 minutes on medium heat until cooked through but not sensitive. Season with sea salt and leave aside to stay warm.

Combine the ground beef, onion powder, garlic powder, and salt; form into two burger patty forms. Heat the coconut oil in a separate section and fry the patties on each side until done to your liking. Kill and save to stay warm.

Use a comparable dish, add a sprinkling of coconut oil (if necessary), and sauté the onions over medium heat until tender. Add the garlic and mushrooms, and increase the force slightly to caramelize the mixture. Cook for 5 minutes then serve.

Egg and Veggie Burrito

 serves: 2   Time: 30 mins   Cook Time: 20 mins

Ingredients

- 4 large eggs
- 1/2 cup diced bell peppers (any color)
- 1/2 cup diced onions
- 1/2 cup diced tomatoes
- 1/2 cup shredded cheese (cheddar, Monterey Jack, or your choice)
- 4 large flour tortillas
- Salt and pepper to taste
- Olive oil or butter for cooking

Directions

Heat olive oil in a pan over medium heat. Add the diced sweet potatoes to the pan and simmer for about 5-7 minutes, then mix until smooth.

Add the chopped onion, red ring pepper, and minced garlic to the pan with the sweet potatoes.

Cook for another 5-7 minutes, or until the veggies are tender and caramelized, combining occasionally.

Season with salt, pepper, and any other desired seasonings, such as paprika or cumin. Blend until it is set.

When everything has been thoroughly cooked and notably burnt, remove it from the flame. Serve the sweet potato hash as a side dish or as a foundation for cooked or poached eggs.

Olive and Rosemary Focaccia

 serves: 2   Time: 30 mins   Cook Time: 20 mins

Ingredients

- 2 cups all-purpose flour
- 1 teaspoon salt
- 1 teaspoon sugar
- 1 teaspoon active dry yeast
- 3/4 cup warm water
- 1/4 cup olive oil, plus extra for drizzling
- 1/4 cup pitted olives, sliced
- 1 tablespoon fresh rosemary, chopped
- Coarse sea salt for sprinkling

Directions

1. Combine the sugar and yeast in a small dish and dissolve in warm water. Allow it to sit for about 5 minutes until it foams.
2. Consolidate the flour and salt in a large mixing basin. Create a well in the center and pour in the yeast mixture and olive oil.
3. Blend until well combined, then knead on a floured surface for 5-7 minutes until the batter is smooth and malleable.
4. Put the mixture in a lubricated bowl, cover it with a beautiful fabric, and let it rise in a warm place for about an hour, or until it has multiplied in size.
5. Preheat the burner to 425°F (220°C). cook for 20 minutes and serve.

# Whole Wheat Pancakes

serves: 2 Time: 30 mins Cook Time: 20 mins

Ingredients

- 1 cup whole wheat flour
- 1 tablespoon sugar (optional)
- 1 teaspoon baking powder
- 1/2 teaspoon baking soda
- 1/4 teaspoon salt
- 1 cup plain Greek yogurt
- 1/2 cup milk (dairy or plant-based)
- 2 large eggs
- 1 teaspoon vanilla extract
- 1 tablespoon olive oil or melted coconut oil
- Fresh fruit (such as berries, figs, or sliced bananas) for topping
- Honey or pure maple syrup for drizzling

Directions

In a large mixing basin, combine the whole wheat flour, sugar (if needed), baking powder, baking soda, and salt.

In another dish, combine the Greek yogurt, milk, eggs, vanilla concentrate, and olive oil until well combined.

Void the wet trims into the dry trimmings and mix until well blended. Be cautious not to overmix; it's fine if there are two or three knocks.

Cook on a nonstick skillet or griddle over medium heat. Gently coat with just enough olive oil or cooking sprinkling.

Pour about 1/4 cup hitter onto the pan for each hotcake. Cook for about 2-3 minutes, or until the bubbles form at a shallow level and the edges seem firm. Flip and heat for a further 1-2 minutes, or until golden brown. Keep the hotcakes warm in a low oven (around 200°F or 95°C) if making different gatherings.

Serve the hotcakes warm, polished off with new verdant food varieties shower of honey or pure maple syrup.

Savory Spinach and Mushroom Oatmeal

serves: 2 Time: 15mins Cook Time: 5mins

Ingredients

- 1 cup rolled oats
- 2 cups water or vegetable broth
- 1 cup fresh spinach, chopped
- 1 cup mushrooms, sliced
- 1 tablespoon olive oil
- 2 cloves garlic, minced
- Salt and pepper to taste
- Optional toppings: grated cheese, chopped herbs, a dash of hot sauce

Directions

Warm up the olive oil in a skillet using a medium setting. Garlic powder should be added and quickly sautéed until aromatic. Cook the chopped mushrooms until they release their moisture and start to turn brown. Cook until shriveled after adding the chopped spinach.

Pour water or vegetable stock into the pan along with the relocated oats. Bring to a gentle simmer, then reduce heat to low and cook, stirring occasionally, for about 5 to 7 minutes, or until the oats are tender and the mixture thickens. Adjust the salt and pepper to your liking.

Serve the ideal combination of spinach and mushrooms hot, then again with a dash of spicy sauce, chopped flavors, or grated cheddar.

MORNING BASIL SKILLET

Ingredients:

- 3 baby bok choy
- 2 bunches spinach
- 1 white sweet potato
- 3 tablespoons extra-virgin olive oil, divided
- 13/4 teaspoons sea salt, divided
- 1 pound ground pork
- 1 teaspoon dried basil
- 1 tablespoon coconut oil

Preparation Steps:

Chop the spinach and bok choy. Cut the sweet potato into 1/3-inch (8 mm) pieces after stripping it, then put it in a basin and add water to cover it (to prevent oxidation).

In a large pan, heat 1 tablespoon (15 ml) olive oil over medium power. Add the bok choy and ¼ teaspoon of salt when it's heated, and simmer for about 6 minutes, or until it becomes tender. After moving to a dish, turn the skillet back on to the heat.

In the skillet, heat an additional 1 tablespoon (15 ml) of olive oil. Once heated, mix in 1/4 teaspoon of salt and sauté the spinach for 2 to 3 minutes, or until it wilts. Transfer to a platter and turn the skillet back on.

Warm up the additional 1 tablespoon (15 milliliters) of olive oil in the skillet. Add the dried basil, 3/4 teaspoon of salt, and the ground pork when it's heated. Stir thoroughly, and cook for 5 to 6 minutes, or until the food is no longer pink. Using an opened spatula, transfer to a platter and discard cooking liquids. Empty the skillet. Take a paper towel and gently clean the sweet potatoes. In the skillet, heat the coconut oil using medium-focused intensity. Once heated, mix in the sweet potatoes along with the remaining ½ teaspoon of salt. Cook, stirring occasionally, for approximately 8 minutes, or until the potatoes are soft and cooked through.

3-2

35 mints

5/10

Quinoa Salad

 serves: 2

 Time: 10 mins

 Cook Time: 0 mins

Ingredients

- 1 cup cooked quinoa
- 1 cup cherry tomatoes, halved
- 1 cup fresh mozzarella balls (or cubed mozzarella)
- 1/4 cup fresh basil leaves, chopped
- 2 tablespoons balsamic vinegar
- 2 tablespoons extra-virgin olive oil
- Salt and pepper to taste

Directions

Combine fresh mozzarella, chopped basil, cooked quinoa, and cherry tomatoes in a large bowl. Drizzle with olive oil and balsamic vinegar.

Use salt and pepper to season according to your taste.

Combine everything till a specific point is reached. Present the chilled Caprese Quinoa Salad.

25

Chickpea Wraps

 serves: 2

 Time: 10 mins

Cook Time: 0 mins

Ingredients

- 1 can chickpeas, drained and rinsed
- 1/2 cup diced cucumber
- 1/2 cup diced tomatoes
- 1/4 cup chopped red onion
- 2 tablespoons chopped fresh parsley
- 2 tablespoons lemon juice
- 2 tablespoons olive oil
- Salt and pepper to taste
- Whole grain wraps or tortillas

Directions

Combine chopped tomatoes, diced cucumber, diced red onion, and fresh parsley in a dish with the chickpeas. Use olive oil and lemon juice as a shower.
Add pepper and salt for seasoning, then thoroughly combine.
Spoon the chickpea mixture onto each warmed wrap or tortilla. Serve the wraps after tightly rolling them up.

Veggie Hummus Wraps

 serves: 2

 Time: 10 mins

Cook Time: 0 mins

Ingredients

- 4 whole grain wraps or tortillas
- 1 cup hummus
- 2 cups mixed fresh vegetables (such as shredded carrots, cucumber slices, bell peppers, lettuce, etc.)
- 1/4 cup crumbled feta cheese (optional)
- 1/4 cup chopped fresh herbs (parsley, cilantro, or basil)
- Salt and pepper to taste

Directions

Lay out the whole tortillas or grain wraps on a perfect surface.
Drizzle each wrap with a generous amount of hummus.
Arrange the mixed fresh veggies on the hummus as well.
Drizzle crumbled feta cheese (if using) and shave fresh herbs over the vegetables. Adjust the salt and pepper to your liking.
When necessary, split the wraps in half and roll them up firmly.
Serve the Veggie Hummus Wraps immediately or cover them with foil for a hearty triumph.

Lunch

LUNCH
RECIPES

Teriyaki Tofu Rice Bowls

 **serves: 2**

 Time: 40 mins

 Cook Time: 20 mins

Ingredients

- 1 block extra-firm tofu, pressed and cubed
- 1/4 cup teriyaki sauce
- 2 cups cooked rice (white or brown)
- 1 cup steamed broccoli florets
- 1/2 cup sliced carrots
- Sesame seeds for garnish
- Green onions, chopped, for garnish

Directions

Set oven temperature to 375°F, or 190°C. Pour the teriyaki sauce over the cubed tofu to coat it evenly. Place the tofu onto a baking sheet covered with parchment paper, and bake for 20 to 25 minutes, or until the tofu is firm.

Build up a rice bowl base of cooked rice, then top with steamed broccoli, chopped carrots, and teriyaki tofu. Add some sesame seeds and chopped green onions as garnish.

Lemon Herb Grilled Chicken Salad

 **serves: 2**

 Time: 30 mins

 Cook Time: 20 mins

Ingredients

- 2 boneless, skinless chicken breasts
- Zest and juice of 1 lemon
- 2 tablespoons olive oil
- 2 cloves garlic, minced
- 1 teaspoon dried thyme
- Salt and pepper to taste
- Mixed salad greens
- Cherry tomatoes, halved
- Cucumber slices
- Red onion slices

Directions

Combine lemon punch, lemon juice, olive oil, dried thyme, minced garlic, salt, and pepper in a bowl. Let the chicken chests sit in the mixture for around half an hour.

Heat the grill or grill dish using a medium-high intensity flame. Chicken chests should be cooked through after grilling for 6 to 8 minutes on each side.

After letting the chicken rest for a few minutes, chop it. Place cucumber slices, red onion slices, cherry tomatoes, and mixed salad greens in a bowl. Sprinkle your preferred salad dressing over the top and add sliced grilled chicken.

Vegan Cauliflower Wings

 serves: 2

⌛ Time: 30 mins

🕐 Cook Time: 10 mins

Ingredients

- 1 head cauliflower, cut into florets
- 1 cup all-purpose flour (or chickpea flour for gluten-free)
- 1 cup plant-based milk
- 1 teaspoon garlic powder
- 1 teaspoon onion powder
- 1/2 teaspoon paprika
- Salt and pepper to taste
- Buffalo sauce or barbecue sauce for coating
- Vegan ranch or blue cheese dressing for dipping

Directions

Adjust oven temperature to 450°F (230°C). Use parchment paper to line a baking sheet.

To create the batter, mix flour, plant-based milk, paprika, onion, garlic, and salt in a bowl.

Make sure the batter is covered by dousing each cauliflower floret with water.

Arrange the battered cauliflower florets in a single layer on the prepared baking sheet.

Place the pan in the hot grill and turn it occasionally for 20 to 25 minutes, or until it looks amazing and fresh.

After removing the cauliflower wings from the oven, thoroughly wash them and coat them with spicy or BBQ sauce.

Warm up some vegan homestead or blue cheddar dressing to dip into these adorable vegetable cauliflower wings.

  # Grilled Chicken Salad

 serves: 2

⌛ Time: 20 mins

🕐 Cook Time: 0 mins

Ingredients

- Grilled chicken breast, sliced
- Mixed salad greens (spinach, arugula, romaine)
- Cherry tomatoes, halved
- Cucumber, sliced
- Avocado, diced
- Red onion, thinly sliced
- Balsamic vinaigrette dressing (olive oil, balsamic vinegar, Dijon mustard, salt, and pepper)

Directions

Add the cherry tomatoes, cucumber, avocado, red onion, and leafy greens to a large bowl.

Place the sliced grilled chicken breast over the bed of lush leaves.

Toss gently to combine, then sprinkle with the balsamic vinaigrette dressing.

Serve right away.

Pesto Chicken Panini

 serves: 2   Time: 15 mins   🕐 Cook Time: 6 mins

Ingredients

- 2 boneless, skinless chicken breasts
- Salt and pepper to taste
- 4 tablespoons basil pesto
- 4 slices mozzarella cheese
- 8 slices bread (ciabatta, focaccia, or your choice)
- Olive oil or butter for grilling

Directions

Add salt and pepper to the chicken chests for seasoning. The chicken chests should be cooked through after 6 to 8 minutes on each side in a grill or pan.

On each slice of bread, spread 1 tablespoon of basil pesto. Place a slice of mozzarella over four of the bread slices.

Cut the cooked chicken breast into pieces, then divide them among the slices of mozzarella. To make sandwiches, place the generous slices of bread, pesto side down, on top.

Prepare a skillet, grill area, or panini press to medium heat. Spread margarine or lightly oil the outside of the sandwiches. Cook the sandwiches until the cheddar is melted and the bread is deliciously hard. Warm Pesto Chicken Panini should be served.

Cauliflower Steaks with Chimichurri Sauce

serves: 2   Time: 30 mins   Cook Time: 20 mins

Ingredients

- 1 large head cauliflower
- 2 tablespoons olive oil
- Salt and pepper to taste

Chimichurri sauce:
- 1 cup fresh parsley, chopped
- 1/4 cup fresh cilantro, chopped
- 2 cloves garlic, minced
- 1/4 cup red wine vinegar
- 1/2 cup olive oil
- Salt and pepper to taste

Directions

Assign 425°F (220°C) as the oven's setting.

With the middle of the cauliflower still whole, remove the outer leaves and cut off the stem end.

Thinly slice the cauliflower into 1-inch-thick steaks.

On a baking sheet covered with parchment paper, arrange the cauliflower steaks.

Lightly oil both sides of the cauliflower steaks, then season with salt & pepper.

Preheat the oven to 200°C. Bake, tossing regularly, for 20 to 25 minutes, or until soft and nicely browned.

Meanwhile, cook the cauliflower and make the chimichurri sauce. In a bowl, mix the olive oil, chopped parsley, minced garlic, red wine vinegar, and cilantro. Season with pepper and salt to taste.

Before serving, move the cooked cauliflower steaks to a platter.

 # Veggie Spring Rolls with Peanut Sauce

 serves: 2   **Time:** 20 mins   🕐 **Cook Time:** 0 mins

Ingredients

- 1/4 cup natural peanut butter
- 2 tablespoons soy sauce or tamari
- 1 tablespoon lime juice
- 1 tablespoon rice vinegar
- 1 tablespoon honey or sugar-free sweetener
- 1 clove garlic, minced
- 1 teaspoon grated ginger
- Water, as needed to thin out the sauce

Directions

Combine peanut butter, soy sauce, ground ginger, lime juice, rice vinegar, honey, or sugar in a small bowl and whisk until well combined.

If the sauce seems too thick, you may thin it out a bit at a time, a tablespoon at a time, until you reach the right consistency.

Adjust the preparation by tasting it and adding extra soy sauce or lime juice as needed.

Transfer the nut sauce to a dish for serving.

Keep the vegetable spring rolls close by so they may be dipped.

 # Turkey Avocado BLT Sandwich

 serves: 2   **Time: 10 mins**   🕐 **Cook Time:** 3 mins

Ingredients

- 8 slices bread (whole grain, white, or your choice)
- 8 slices cooked bacon
- 8 slices roasted turkey breast
- 1 ripe avocado, sliced
- 4 lettuce leaves
- 2 tomatoes, sliced
- Mayonnaise or your preferred spread

Directions

When desired, toast the bread slices. On one side of each slice of bread, add mayonnaise or your favorite spread.

Arrange the slices of bacon, avocado, tomato, lettuce, and simmering turkey breast on four slices of bread.

Place the remaining 4 slices of bread on top to create a sandwich frame. When ready to serve, slant the sandwiches along the center and cut them.

Chicken Tomatoes

 serves: 2   **Time: 25 mins**   🕐 **Cook Time:** 5mins

Ingredients

- 1 pound boneless, skinless chicken ribcage, created due
- 1 cup low-sodium poultry stock
- 2 medium tomatoes, cut 1 medium onion, split and minced
- Punch and crush of 1 lemon
- 1 teaspoon herbes de Provence
- ½ teaspoon salt
- ½ teaspoon powdered pepper
- ⅓ cup quartered mild or green olives
- 2 tablespoons trimmed new parsley

Directions

The bread slices can be toasted anytime desired. On one side of every piece of bread, add mayonnaise or your favorite spread. Arrange the cooked turkey breast, bacon, avocado, lettuce, and tomato slices on four slices of bread.

Add the remaining four slices of bread on top to frame partition a turkey breast into four equal halves. In a 6-quart slow cooker, combine the chicken, stock, shallots, tomatoes, lemon juice, Provence seasonings, lemon blended drink, salt, and pepper. Cook on High for 1 hour and 30 minutes, or on Low for 3 hours and 30 minutes. Stir in the olives and simmer, covered, until the orzo is tender, about 30 minutes more. Give in to a reasonable settlement. Before serving, distribute some

Salmon Couscous Salad

 serves: 2   **Time: 10 mins**   **Cook Time:** 0 mins

Ingredients

- ¼ cup diced cremini mushrooms
- ¼ cup minced aubergine
- 3 cups neonatal spinach
- 2 tablespoons white-wine vinaigrette, divided
- ¼ cup cooked Israeli couscous, ideally whole-wheat
- 4 ounces broiled salmon
- ¼ cup sliced dried apricots
- 2 tablespoons grated goat cheese (1/2 ounce)

> To make the most mouth-watering salmon you've ever tasted, all you need is 200 degrees for 14 minutes in the oven or a skillet until golden.

Directions

Put a cooking spray on a small skillet and heat it over medium heat. Add the eggplant and mushrooms; cook, stirring, for 3 to 5 minutes, or until the eggplant is just sautéed and the liquids are transferred. Release the force and put it down.

Pour 1 tablespoon plus 1 teaspoon of vinaigrette over the spinach and arrange on a 9-inch dish.

After tossing the couscous with a generous amount of 2 tsp. vinaigrette, arrange it over the spinach. Place salmon on top. Add the goat cheddar and defended apricots to the top of the sautéed veggies.

32

Quinoa Power Salad

🍽 serves: 2   ⧖ Time: 20 mins   🕐 Cook Time: 10 mins

Ingredients

- 1 medium sweet potato
- ½ red onion, sliced into 1/4-inch-thick pieces
- 2 teaspoons extra-virgin olive oil, disconnected
- ½ teaspoon garlic powder
- ¼ teaspoon salt, divided
- 8 ounces poultry tenders
- 2 tablespoons whole grain mustard, divided
- 1 tablespoon finely hacked shallot
- 1 teaspoons unadulterated maple syrup
- 1 tablespoon juice vinegar
- 4 cups immature greens
- ½ cup cooked red quinoa, cooled
- 1 tablespoon unsalted sunflower seeds, toasted

Directions

Preheat the oven to 425 degrees. In a medium-sized bowl, mix the sweet potatoes, onion, 1 tablespoon oil, 1/8 teaspoon salt, and garlic powder. Spread out onto a large baking sheet and bake at high heat for 15 minutes.

Meanwhile, put the chicken in a dish with 1 tablespoon mustard and toss to coat. Remove from the oven and toss the veggies after they have simmered for fifteen minutes. Put the chicken inside the container. Return the casserole to the oven and simmer for an additional ten minutes, or until the vegetables are starting to caramelize and the chicken is well cooked. Take the grill off and let it cool.

Meanwhile, mix the shallot, vinegar, and maple syrup.

Chicken Nuggets

 serves: 2   ⧖ Time: 30 mins   🕐 Cook Time: 0 mins

Ingredients

- Boneless, skinless chicken breasts, cut into bite-sized pieces
- 1 cup breadcrumbs (use whole wheat or gluten-free breadcrumbs for a healthier option)
- 1/2 cup grated Parmesan cheese
- 1 teaspoon garlic powder
- 1 teaspoon onion powder
- Salt and pepper, to taste
- 2 eggs, beaten
- Cooking spray or olive oil

Directions

Preheat your broiler to 400 degrees Fahrenheit (200 degrees Celsius). Line a baking sheet with material paper and lightly oil with cooking spray or olive oil.

In a small bowl, mix together breadcrumbs, ground Parmesan cheddar, garlic powder, onion powder, salt, and pepper.

Dip each chicken piece into the beaten eggs, then coat evenly with the breadcrumb mixture.

Place the wrapped chicken tenders on the pre-arranged baking sheet.

Heat on a preheated broiler for 15-20 minutes, turning halfway through, until the chicken is cooked through and the coating is bright and firm.

Serve these locally crafted chicken strips with ketchup, grill sauce, or honey mustard for dipping.

Vegan Vegetable Nuggets

🍽 serves: 2   ⏳ Time: 40 mins   🕐 Cook Time: 20 mins

Ingredients

- 2 cups mixed vegetables (such as carrots, peas, corn, and broccoli), finely chopped or grated
- 1 cup cooked quinoa or brown rice
- 1/2 cup breadcrumbs (whole wheat or gluten-free)
- 1/4 cup nutritional yeast
- 2 tablespoons ground flaxseeds + 6 tablespoons water (flaxseed "egg")
- 2 cloves garlic, minced
- 1 teaspoon onion powder
- 1/2 teaspoon smoked paprika
- Salt and pepper to taste
- Olive oil or cooking spray for greasing

Directions

Turn the oven on to 375°F, or 190°C. A baking sheet should be lined with parchment paper and lightly oiled with cooking spray or olive oil.

Combine the ground flaxseeds and water in a small dish to form a flaxseed "egg." Allow it to thicken for about five minutes.

Combine the finely chopped or crushed veggies, cooked quinoa or hearty colored rice, breadcrumbs, active yeast, smoked paprika, onion powder, minced garlic, salt, and flaxseed "egg" in a large mixing bowl.

Using your hands, bring everything together until it's mostly all together. When pushed, the mixture ought to stay together.

Using your hands, take little portions of the mixture and form them into lumpy pieces. Transfer the parts to the prepared baking sheet. When all of the pieces have been created, carefully coat the tops with olive oil or a frying sprinkle. This will help them crisp up in the oven.

Cook the vegetable pieces in the preheated oven for 25-30 minutes, flipping halfway through, until they are golden brown and firm.

Once finished, remove the pieces from the oven and allow them to cool for a few minutes before serving.

Shrimp and Avocado Wraps

🍽 serves: 2   ⏳ Time: 30 mins   🕐 Cook Time: 10 mins

Ingredients

- 1 pound cooked shrimp, peeled and deveined
- 1 ripe avocado, diced
- 1/4 cup red onion, finely chopped
- 1/4 cup cucumber, diced
- 1/4 cup bell pepper, diced
- 2 tablespoons fresh cilantro, chopped
- Juice of 1 lime
- Salt and pepper to taste
- Lettuce leaves or tortillas for wrapping

Directions

In a mixing bowl, add the cooked shrimp, avocado, finely sliced red onion, cucumber, bell pepper, cilantro, lime juice, salt, and pepper. Mix carefully. Taste and adjust the seasoning as required.

If using lettuce leaves, spread the shrimp and avocado mixture over the leaves and fold them up to form wraps. If using tortillas, spread the mixture onto the tortillas, fold in the edges, and roll into wraps.

Immediately serve the Shrimp and Avocado Salad Wraps.

Beef Lettuce Wraps

serves: 2   Time: 15 mins   Cook Time: 2 mins

Ingredients

- Lean ground beef
- Garlic, minced
- Onion, diced
- Bell peppers, diced
- Low-sodium soy sauce
- Sesame oil
- Lettuce leaves (such as iceberg or butter lettuce)
- Optional toppings: chopped green onions, sesame seeds

Directions

In a pan, caramelize a lean ground beef with chopped garlic and sliced onion.

Cook diced ringer peppers in the skillet till delicate.

Season with low-sodium soy sauce and sesame oil.

Spoon the hamburger mixture over lettuce leaves and garnish with sliced green onions and sesame seeds as desired.

Roll up the lettuce leaves and fasten them with toothpicks. Serve straight away.

Sweet Potato and Black Bean Enchiladas with Avocado

serves: 2   Time: 30 mins   Cook Time: 20 mins

Ingredients

- 4 large lettuce leaves (for low-carb option) or low-carb tortillas
- 1 cup cooked sweet potato, mashed
- 1 cup canned black beans, drained and rinsed
- 1/4 cup diced onion
- 1/4 cup diced bell pepper
- 1/4 cup enchilada sauce (choose a low-carb option)
- 1/4 cup shredded cheese (choose a low-fat option if preferred)
- Sliced avocado for topping

Directions

Preheat your stove to 375°F.

In a blender, combine the smashed yam, dark beans, chopped onion, and diced ringer pepper.

Spoon the yam-dark bean mixture onto each lettuce leaf or low-carb tortilla.

Roll the lettuce leaves or tortillas and place them crease-side down in a baking tray.

Pour enchilada sauce over the enchiladas and top with the crumbled cheddar.

Cover the baking dish with foil and cook on the preheated burner for 20-25 minutes, or until warmed through and the cheddar has liquefied.

Remove from the heat and top with chopped avocado before serving.

Egg Foo Young

 serves: 2 Time: 10 mins 🕐 Cook Time: 5 mins

Ingredients

- 4 eggs
- 1/2 cup cooked chicken, shrimp, or pork (optional)
- 1/4 cup bean sprouts
- 1/4 cup diced onion
- 1/4 cup diced bell pepper
- 1/4 cup sliced mushrooms
- 1/4 cup chopped green onions
- 2 tablespoons soy sauce
- Salt and pepper to taste
- Oil for frying

Directions

To prepare Egg Foo Youthful, begin by assembling your ingredients: Cook and dice 1/2 cup chicken, shrimp, or pork whenever desired. Dice 1/4 cup each of onion, bell pepper, and mushrooms, and chop 1/4 cup green onions. In a large mixing bowl, beat 4 eggs and add the meat (if using), 1/4 cup bean sprouts, chopped veggies, and green onions. Season with 2 tablespoons soy sauce, salt, and pepper, to taste. Heat a little amount of oil in a large skillet over medium heat. Pour a ladleful of egg mixture into the pan, forming a small patty. Cook for approximately 2-3 minutes per side, or until golden brown and heated through. Rehash with the remaining mix. Serve

Black Bean and Corn Quesadillas with Guacamole

 serves: 2 ⏳ Time: 15mins Cook Time: 5 mins

Ingredients

- 2 low-carb tortillas
- 1/2 cup canned black beans, drained and rinsed
- 1/4 cup canned corn kernels, drained
- 1/4 cup shredded cheese (choose a low-fat option if preferred)
- 1/4 cup guacamole (homemade or store-bought)
- Optional toppings: salsa, Greek yogurt (as a sour cream substitute), chopped cilantro

Directions

Heat a nonstick skillet over medium heat.
Place one tortilla in the skillet and cover it with half of the crumbled cheddar.
Spoon half of the dark beans and corn onto the cheddar.
Sprinkle with the remaining destroyed cheddar and top with the next tortilla.
Cook the tortillas for 2-3 minutes on each side, or until they are golden brown and the cheddar has melted.
Remove from the skillet and let cool slightly before cutting into wedges.
Serve hot, with guacamole and optional toppings as an afterthought.

Grilled Salmon with Roasted Vegetables

 serves: 4   Time: 15 mins   Cook Time: 20 mins

Ingredients

- 4 salmon fillets (6 oz each)
- 1 lemon, zested and juiced
- 2 cloves garlic, minced
- 1 tablespoon fresh thyme, chopped
- 1 tablespoon extra virgin olive oil
- Salt and black pepper to taste
- 1 large sweet potato, peeled and cubed
- 1 red bell pepper, cut into chunks
- 1 yellow squash, sliced
- 1 zucchini, sliced
- 1 tablespoon olive oil
- Dried oregano
- Dried basil

Directions

Marinate the Salmon: In a small bowl, combine lemon zest, juice, garlic, thyme, olive oil, salt, and pepper. Massage the marinade into the salmon fillets and let them rest for at least 15 minutes.

Prepare the Vegetables: Preheat oven to 400°F (200°C). Toss sweet potato, bell pepper, squash, and zucchini with olive oil, oregano, and basil. Season with salt and pepper.

Grill the Salmon: Preheat your grill to medium-high heat. Grill the salmon fillets for about 5-7 minutes per side, or until cooked through.

Roast the Vegetables: While the salmon is grilling, roast the vegetables for 20-25 minutes, or until tender and slightly caramelized.

Serve: Place a portion of roasted vegetables on each plate and top with a grilled salmon fillet. Garnish with additional fresh thyme, if desired.

Creamy Garlic Parmesan Pasta

serves: 2   Time: 30 mins   Cook Time: 20 mins

Ingredients

- 8 ounces of pasta (such as spaghetti, fettuccine, or your preferred type)
- 2 tablespoons of butter
- 4 cloves of minced garlic
- 1 cup of heavy cream
- 1/2 cup of grated Parmesan cheese
- Salt and pepper for seasoning, to taste
- Optional garnish: chopped parsley

Directions

Set up the pasta according to the instructions on the package. Channel and store it away. Soften the margarine in a container set to medium heat. Sauté the minced garlic until it is aromatic.

Pour in the heavy cream, bringing it to a simmer to slightly thicken. Stir in the ground Parmesan cheddar until it liquefies and the sauce thickens.

Season with salt and pepper. Add the cooked pasta to the sauce, making sure it's evenly distributed. Alternatively, garnish with sliced parsley before serving.

DINNER

Dinner

DINNER
RECIPES

Classic Lasagna with Beef

 serves: 2

Ingredients

- 1lb of ground beef
- 1 onion, sliced
- 3 cloves of finely chopped garlic
- 1 tomatoe, chopped
- Nine noodles
- 1⁄2 cup of ricotta cheese
- 2 cups of shredded mozzarella cheese
- 1 cup of finely chopped Parmesan cheese
- Add the dry herbs (oregano, basil) and salt and pepper to taste.

 Time: 40 mins

Directions

Brown the beef with garlic and onion. Combine the spices, salt, pepper, and smashed tomatoes. Let it simmer for 20 minutes.
Set the stove to 375°F. Cook the lasagna noodles according to the bundle's instructions.
Combine the noodles, sauce, mozzarella, ricotta, and Parmesan in a baking dish. Rehash two times.
Prepare for 25 minutes with a foil lid on.
After a further 25 minutes of baking, uncover it and let it boil. Allow 10 minutes to decompress. Warm up and serve.

Teriyaki Glazed Salmon

 serves: 2

Ingredients

- 4 pieces of salmon fillet
- 1/4 cup of soy sauce
- 2 tablespoons of honey
- 1 tablespoon of rice vinegar
- 1 tablespoon of sesame oil
- 2 cloves of minced garlic
- 1 teaspoon of grated ginger
- Optional garnish: sesame seeds and chopped green onions

 Time: 30 mins   Cook Time: 20 mins

Directions

Mix soy sauce, honey, rice vinegar, sesame oil, chopped garlic, and ground ginger in a bowl. Marinate the salmon fillets in this mixture for 15-30 minutes. Preheat the broiler to 400 degrees Fahrenheit (200 degrees Celsius) and line a baking sheet with material paper. Place the marinated salmon on a baking sheet and bake for 12-15 minutes, or until well cooked and easily chipped with a fork. While baking, brush the fish with the extra marinade intermittently.
Alternatively, before serving, top with sesame seeds and sliced green onions.

Ratatouille

 serves: 2   Time: 40 mins   🕐 Cook Time: 25 mins

Ingredients

- 1 eggplant, diced
- 2 zucchinis, diced
- 2 bell peppers (red and yellow), diced
- 4 tomatoes, diced
- 1 onion, chopped
- 3 cloves garlic, minced
- 2 tablespoons tomato paste
- 2 tablespoons olive oil
- 1 teaspoon dried thyme
- 1 teaspoon dried basil
- Salt and pepper to taste
- Fresh basil leaves for garnish

Directions

1. Prep the vegetables: Cut the eggplant, zucchini, bell peppers, tomatoes, onion, and garlic into the desired sizes.
2. Sauté the vegetables: Heat olive oil in a large skillet over medium heat. Add the onion and sauté until softened. Add the garlic and cook for an additional minute.
3. Add the vegetables: Stir in the eggplant, zucchini, bell peppers, and tomatoes. Season with salt, pepper, thyme, and basil.
4. Simmer: Reduce heat to low and simmer for 25-30 minutes, or until the vegetables are tender.
5. Add tomato paste: Stir in the tomato paste and cook for 5 minutes more.
6. Serve: Serve immediately, garnished with fresh basil leaves. Enjoy your delicious ratatouille!

Shrimp Pad Thai

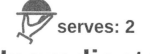 serves: 2   Time: 30 mins   🕐 Cook Time: 20 mins

Ingredients

- 8 ounces of rice noodles
- 1 pound of shrimp, peeled and deveined
- 2 tablespoons of vegetable oil
- 3 cloves of minced garlic
- 2 lightly beaten eggs
- 1 cup of bean sprouts
- 1/2 cup of chopped green onions
- 1/4 cup of chopped peanuts
- Lime wedges for serving

Directions

Begin by cooking the rice noodles according to the package directions, then channel and store them. To prepare the Cushion Thai sauce, combine fish sauce, tamarind glue, earthy-colored sugar, rice vinegar, and bean stew chips in a dish.

Heat the oil in a large wok or pan over medium-high heat. Pan-sear the minced garlic and shrimp until they are pink.

Push the shrimp aside from the pan and pour the beaten eggs on the other side. Scramble the eggs until cooked, then combine them with the shrimp.

Throw the cooked noodles and Cushion Thai sauce into the wok, making sure everything is well coated. Cook for a few minutes more after adding the bean sprouts and sliced green onions.

Serve the meal hot while decorating.

Cauliflower "Steak" with Chimichurri Sauce

serves: 2   Time: 30 mins   Cook Time: 10 mins

Ingredients

- 1 head cauliflower, sliced into "steaks"
- 2 tablespoons olive oil
- Salt and pepper to taste
- For the chimichurri sauce:
- 1/2 cup fresh parsley, chopped
- 2 tablespoons fresh cilantro, chopped
- 2 cloves garlic, minced
- 1/4 cup red wine vinegar
- 1/2 cup extra virgin olive oil
- Salt and pepper to taste

Directions

Set the stove to 425°F (220°C). Line a baking sheet with parchment paper.
Place the cauliflower "steaks" on a prepared baking sheet. Sprinkle with olive oil and season with salt and pepper.

Broil for 25-30 minutes on a hot burner until the cauliflower is delicate and golden brown.
Prepare the chimichurri sauce while the cauliflower is broiling. Combine hacked parsley, chopped cilantro, minced garlic, red wine vinegar, and extra virgin olive oil in a bowl. Season with salt and pepper as desired.
Serve the broiled cauliflower "steaks" hot and drenched in chimichurri sauce.

Spinach and Artichoke Stuffed Portobello Mushrooms

serves: 2   Time: 30 mins   Cook Time: 10 mins

Ingredients

- 4 large portobello mushrooms, stems removed
- 2 cups chopped spinach
- 1 cup chopped artichoke hearts
- 1/2 cup vegan cream cheese
- 1/4 cup nutritional yeast
- 2 cloves garlic, minced
- Salt and pepper to taste

Directions

Preheat your stove to 375°F (190°C). Line a baking sheet with material paper.
Place the portobello mushrooms on the pre-arranged baking sheet, and gill side up.
In a mixing dish, combine chopped spinach, sliced artichoke hearts, vegetable lover cream cheddar, healthy yeast, minced garlic, salt, and pepper.
Spoon the spinach and artichoke mixture into each portobello mushroom cap.
Cook on a hot burner for 20-25 minutes, or until the mushrooms are tender and the filling has warmed through.
Serve hot as a delightful and satisfying hors d'oeuvre or main meal.

Vegan Stuffed Bell Peppers with Rice and Beans

serves: 2 **Time: 30 mins** **Cook Time:** 10 mins

Ingredients

- 4 bell peppers, halved and seeds removed
- 1 cup cooked rice (white or brown)
- 1 can (15 oz) black beans, drained and rinsed
- 1 cup diced tomatoes
- 1/2 cup corn kernels (fresh or frozen)
- 1/2 cup diced onion
- 2 cloves garlic, minced
- 1 teaspoon ground cumin
- 1 teaspoon chili powder
- Salt and pepper to taste
- Vegan shredded cheese for topping (optional)
- Fresh cilantro for garnish

Directions

Preheat the broiler to 375° F (190° C). Oil a baking dish or spray it with cooking spray.

Place the split ringer peppers in the pre-arranged baking dish.

In a large bowl, combine cooked rice, black beans, diced tomatoes, corn kernels, diced onion, minced garlic, ground cumin, stew powder, salt, and pepper.

Spoon the rice and bean mixture into each ringer pepper half, pressing down gently to pack it.

Cover the baking dish with foil and broil for 30–35 minutes, or until the ringer peppers are delicate.

If you are using vegetarian destroyed cheddar, remove the foil and sprinkle it over the filled peppers during the last 5 minutes of baking.

Serve the vegetarian-stuffed ringer peppers hot, garnished with fresh cilantro.

Spinach & White Bean Soup

serves: 2 **Time: 40 mins** **Cook Time:** 20 mins

Ingredients

- 1 tbsp olive oil
- 1 onion, finely chopped
- 2 garlic cloves, minced
- 4 cups vegetable or chicken broth
- 2 cans (15 oz each) white beans, drained
- 4 cups fresh spinach, chopped
- 1 tsp dried thyme
- Salt, pepper, and red pepper flakes to taste
- Grated Parmesan cheese (optional garnish)

Directions

In a saucepan, heat olive oil to a medium temperature. Sauté onions till translucent, then add garlic and simmer for another second.

Pour in stock, add white beans, spinach, thyme, and season with salt, pepper, and red pepper chips.

Stew for 15-20 minutes, allowing the flavors to combine.

Remove from heat, discard any sound leaves, and serve. Alternatively, garnish with Parmesan cheddar before serving.

Garlic Parmesan Crusted Salmon

2   20 mints   6/10

Ingredients:

- 2 lb Salmon fillet
- 1 1/2 tbsp Olive oil
- 1 tbsp Lemon juice
- 1/2 tsp Sea salt
- 1/2 tsp Black pepper
- 1/2 cup Grated parmesan cheese
- 2 tbsp Fresh parsley (chopped)
- 2 tbsp Fresh dill (chopped)
- 1 tsp Garlic powder
- 1 tbsp Unsalted butter (melted

Preparation Steps:

Preheat the oven to 400 °F (204 °C). Line a baking sheet with aluminum foil or parchment paper.

Place the fish on a baking sheet that has been lined. Drizzle olive oil and lemon juice over the fish. Season both sides with sea salt and pepper.

In a small mixing bowl, combine the Parmesan cheese, parsley, dill, and garlic powder. Incorporate the melted butter and whisk until crumbly. Spread the mixture evenly over the fish and press down lightly.

Bake for 10-15 minutes, depending on fish thickness, until easily flaked with a fork.

Crusted White Fish

7-8   cook   45 mints   7/10

Ingredients:

- 2 white fish
- 1 Tablespoon olive oil , or oil spray
- 1/2 cup grated parmesan cheese
- kosher salt , to taste
- black pepper , to taste
- 1/2 teaspoon garlic powder
- 1/2 teaspoon onion powder
- 1/2 teaspoon smoked paprika
- fresh chopped parsley , for garnish
- lemon wedges

Preparation Steps:

Preheat the Air Fryer to 380°F (193°C) for 5 minutes. Place the parmesan in a shallow basin and store it.

Pour liberal amounts of olive oil over the fish or splash it with oil. Season with salt, pepper, garlic, onion, and paprika. Press the fish filets into the cheddar mixture, coating both sides. If you feel the cheddar could stick better, soak the fish in a beaten egg before pressing it into the cheese. The egg will provide more calories.

Line the air fryer basket or plate with pierced material paper. Use an oil shower to delicately spray material paper. Lay the wrapped fish on the material. Daintily spray oil onto the highest point of the fish filets.

Fish Taco Bowls with Cilantro Lime Cream Sauce

Ingredients:

2-3

- 1 Tbls Avocado Oil or oil of choice
- 4 filets Tilpia or fish of choice
- 2 Tbls Cilantro chopped
- 4 Limes
- 1.5 tsp Salt divided
- 1/2 tsp Cumin
- 1/2 Tbls Chili Powder
- 1/4 tsp Cayenne
- 1/4 tsp Garlic Powder
- 1/2 cup Mayo Primal Kitchen
- 2 cups Green Cabbage shredded

cooking

Preparation Steps:

30 mints

In a medium bowl, combine the cabbage, the juice of two limes, and 1/2 tsp salt. Combine as one and save.

In a small bowl, combine the mayo, the juice of one lime, and two tablespoons of chopped cilantro.

Combine the remaining seasonings in a small bowl (salt, stew powder, garlic powder, cumin, and cayenne). Wipe off the fish with a paper towel and coat it with the seasoning combination on both sides.

Heat the avocado oil in a pan over medium heat. When the oil is heated, add the fish and cook for 3-4 minutes on one side before flipping and cooking for an additional 3-4 minutes.

(Cooking time will vary depending on the size of the fish.

5/10

Fish Tacos

3-4

cooking

30 mints

Ingredients:

- 3 salmon fillets 360g / 12.7oz, or a white fish such as cod or flounder
- 2 tablespoon olive oil
- Juice of ½ lime
- ½ teaspoon paprika powder
- ½ teaspoon mild chilli powder
- ½ teaspoon garlic powder
- salt and pepper to taste
- Slaw
- 1 avocado diced
- ½ cup red cabbage shredded
- 1 cup white cabbage shredded
- 1 tablespoon coriander chopped
- 2 spring onions / scallions chopped
- Salsa Dressing
- 1 tablespoon olive oil
- 3 tablespoon coriander chopped
- 1 garlic clove minced
- Juice of ½ lime
- ⅓ cup Greek yoghurt
- ½ jalapeño or to taste

Preparation Steps:

Preheat the Air Fryer to 380°F (193°C) for 5 minutes. Place the parmesan in a shallow basin and store. Pour liberal amounts of olive oil over the fish or splash it with oil. Season with salt, pepper, garlic, onion, and paprika. Press the fish filets into the cheddar mixture, coating both sides. If you feel the cheddar could stick better, soak the fish in beaten egg before pressing it into the cheese. The egg will provide more calories.

Line the air fryer basket or plate with pierced material paper. Use an oil shower to delicately spray material paper. Lay the wrapped fish on the material. Daintily spray oil onto the highest point of the fish filets.

Crust Pizza with Tomato Sauce and Veggies

 serves: 2   Time: 30 mins   Cook Time: 25 mins

Ingredients

- 1 medium cauliflower head, grated (or 2 cups cauliflower rice)
- 1/4 cup almond flour
- 1/4 cup grated Parmesan cheese
- 1 teaspoon Italian seasoning
- 1/2 teaspoon garlic powder
- Salt and pepper to taste
- 1/4 cup tomato sauce (choose a low-carb option)
- 1/4 cup shredded mozzarella cheese (or vegan cheese)
- Sliced vegetables of your choice (e.g., bell peppers, mushrooms, onions, spinach)

Directions

Preheat the burner to 400°F (200°C). Line a baking sheet with material paper.

Place the ground cauliflower in a microwave-safe basin and cook for 5 minutes until softened.

Allow the cauliflower to cool, then lay it in a perfect kitchen towel and press out any excess moisture.

Transfer the cauliflower to a mixing bowl. Combine almond flour, ground Parmesan cheddar, Italian seasoning, garlic powder, salt, and pepper. Blend until everything is combined.

Spread the cauliflower mixture onto the prepared baking sheet, forming it into a round pizza hull.

Place under the preheated broiler for 20-25 minutes, or until the topping is golden brown and firm.

Remove the exterior of the stove and distribute pureed tomatoes evenly on the surface.

Sprinkle the crushed mozzarella cheddar over the sauce.

Slow-Cooker Chicken and Orzo with Tomatoes and Olives

 serves: 2   Time: 25 mins   Cook Time: 20 mins

Ingredients

- 1 pound boneless, skinless chicken ribcage, created due
- 1 cup low-sodium poultry stock
- 2 medium tomatoes, cut 1 medium onion, split and minced
- Punch and squeeze of 1 lemon
- 1 teaspoon herbes de Provence
- ½ teaspoon salt
- ½ teaspoon powdered pepper
- ¾ cup complete wheat orzo
- ⅓ cup quartered pale or green olives
- 2 tablespoons trimmed new parsley

Directions

Every turkey bosom should be sliced in four halves. In a 6-quart slow cooker, combine the chicken, stock, tomatoes, onion, lemonade, lemon juice, herbes de Provence, salt, and pepper. Cook for one hour and 30 minutes on high or three hours and 30 minutes on low. Combine the orzo and olives; cover and simmer for another 30 minutes, or until the orzo is tender. Allow to significantly cool. Sprinkle with parsley right before serving.

Chow Mein

 serves: 2

Time: 40 mins

Cook Time: 20 mins

Ingredients

- 8 oz (225g) chow mein noodles or egg noodles
- 2 tablespoons vegetable oil
- 2 cloves garlic, minced
- 1 onion, sliced
- 1 bell pepper, sliced
- 1 cup shredded cabbage
- 1 cup bean sprouts
- 1 carrot, julienned
- 1/2 cup sliced mushrooms (optional)
- 1/4 cup soy sauce
- 2 tablespoons oyster sauce
- 1 tablespoon sesame oil
- 1 tablespoon rice vinegar
- 1 tablespoon brown sugar
- Cooked protein of your choice (sliced chicken, beef, shrimp, tofu)

Directions

Cook the chow mein noodles as directed on the package. After draining, set away.

Heat the vegetable oil in a big pan or wok over medium-high heat. Add the onion slices and minced garlic. Sauté for a short while until aromatic. Include the sliced bell pepper, julienned carrot, bean sprouts, shredded cabbage or bok choy, and sliced mushrooms, if desired. The veggies should be crisp yet just slightly soft after a few minutes of sautéing.

Stir-fry the cooked protein into the veggies until it is thoroughly hot.

Combine the soy sauce, oyster sauce, sesame oil, rice vinegar, and brown sugar (if using) in a small bowl.

Drizzle the protein and vegetable mixture with the sauce. To coat everything equally, stir.

Combine the cooked chow mein noodles with the sauce in the pan and stir everything around until the noodles are well heated and covered with sauce.

If needed, adjust the seasoning. According to your taste, you can add extra soy sauce or other spices. Present the hot chow mein with the option to top it with sesame seeds or chopped green onions.

Ground Beef Gyros

 serves: 2   Time: 40 mins   Cook Time: 20 mins

Ingredients

- 1 pound ground beef
- 1 small onion, finely chopped
- 3 cloves garlic, minced
- 1 teaspoon dried oregano
- 1 teaspoon paprika
- 1 teaspoon ground cumin
- Salt and pepper to taste
- Pita bread or flatbread
- Tzatziki sauce
- Sliced tomatoes, cucumbers, red onions (for topping)
- Optional: Chopped parsley, crumbled feta cheese

Directions

In a dish, saute the ground hamburger over medium heat until seared. If required, channel any excess fat.

Add chopped onion and garlic to the hamburger. Cook until the onions are transparent.

Season with dried oregano, paprika, ground cumin, salt, and pepper. Mix thoroughly to solidify.

Warm the pita bread. Spoon the meat mixture onto the pita bread.

Tzatziki sauce, sliced tomatoes, cucumbers, red onions, hacked parsley, and crumbled feta cheese can be added as desired.

Roll up the pita and serve your handcrafted Ground Hamburger Gyros.

Spaghetti Carbonara

 serves: 2   Time: 30 mins   Cook Time: 20 mins

Ingredients

- 12 oz spaghetti
- 4-6 slices of bacon or pancetta, diced
- 3 cloves garlic, minced
- 3 large eggs
- 1 cup grated Parmesan cheese
- Salt and black pepper to taste
- Chopped parsley for garnish (optional)

Directions

Cook spaghetti in salted boiling water according to package guidelines until slightly firm. Channel, reserving 1/2 cup spaghetti water.

While the pasta is cooking, broil the chopped bacon in a pan over medium heat until firm. Sauté for 1-2 minutes with minced garlic.

In a mixing dish, combine the eggs, ground Parmesan cheddar, salt, and black pepper.

Place the cooked spaghetti in the pan with the bacon and garlic. Avoid heat.

Pour the egg and cheddar mixture over the heated pasta, tossing frequently to coat. The leftover heat will cook the eggs, yielding a thick sauce. If the pasta is extremely dry, add a small amount of water at a time.

Add hacked parsley and additional ground Parmesan cheddar whenever desired.

Mushroom Chicken Rice Skillet

 serves: 2

 Time: 50 mins

Cook Time: 20 mins

Ingredients

- 1 pound boneless, skinless chicken breasts, cut into bite-sized pieces
- Salt and pepper to taste
- 2 tablespoons olive oil
- 8 oz (225g) mushrooms, sliced
- 1 onion, chopped
- 2 cloves garlic, minced
- 1 cup long-grain white rice
- 2 cups chicken broth
- 1 teaspoon dried thyme
- 1/2 teaspoon paprika
- 1/2 cup grated Parmesan cheese
- Chopped fresh parsley for garnish (optional)

Directions

Add salt and pepper to the chicken pieces for seasoning.
In a big skillet set over medium-high heat, warm up the olive oil. Once added, grill the chicken until it is browned all over. After removing it from the pan, set the chicken aside.
Add chopped onion and sliced mushrooms to the same skillet. Add the onions and sauté for a few minutes, or until the onions become translucent and the mushrooms shed their moisture.
When aromatic, add the minced garlic to the pan and heat for an additional minute.
Add the rice and simmer, stirring, for a few minutes, until it starts to toast.
Add the paprika, dried thyme, and chicken broth. Mix well, being sure to scrape off any browned pieces from the skillet's bottom.
For about 15 to 18 minutes, or until the rice is cooked and the liquid has been absorbed, cover the skillet and simmer the rice.
Stir everything together and add the cooked chicken back to the skillet once the rice is done.
After adding grated Parmesan cheese to the mixture, stir it until it melts and blends.

49

Beef and Broccoli Stir-Fry

serves: 2   **Time: 40 mins**   **Cook Time:** 20 mins

Ingredients

- 1 lb beef sirloin or flank steak, thinly sliced
- 3 cups broccoli florets
- 3 tablespoons soy sauce
- 2 tablespoons oyster sauce
- 2 tablespoons brown sugar
- 2 cloves garlic, minced
- 1 teaspoon grated ginger
- 2 tablespoons vegetable oil
- Sesame seeds for garnish (optional)
- Cooked rice for serving

Directions

Combine soy sauce, brown sugar, oyster sauce, chopped garlic, and grated ginger in a bowl.

Vegetable oil should be heated on high heat in a pan or wok. After adding the beef slices, stir-fry them until browned. Take out and place aside from the pan.

Stir-fry broccoli florets in the same pan for 2 to 3 minutes, or until they become bright green and somewhat tender.

Place the steak back into the pan and cover it with the sauce along with the broccoli. After everything is coated and well cooked, stir-fry for an additional one to two minutes.

If desired, garnish with sesame seeds. With cooked rice, serve hot.

Italian Wedding Soup

serves: 2   **Time: 35 mins**   **Cook Time:** 20 mins

Ingredients

- 4 Tablespoons extra-virgin olive oil
- 1⅓ Cups chopped yellow onion
- ⅔ Cup chopped carrot
- ⅔ Cup chopped celery
- 2 Tablespoons minced garlic
- 6 Cups unsalted chicken broth
- 6 Ounces orzo, preferably whole-wheat
- 1½ Tablespoons chopped fresh oregano
- ½ Teaspoon kosher salt
- 24 Cooked chicken meatballs (12 ounces)
- 4 Cups baby spinach
- ¼ Cup grated Parmesan cheese

Directions

In a big saucepan over medium-high heat, warm up 1 tablespoon of oil.

Incorporate the onion, carrot, celery, and garlic; stir-fry for 4 to 5 minutes, or until the onion becomes transparent.

Pour in the broth, cover, and heat through.

Combine the orzo, salt, and oregano; simmer, covered, turning occasionally, until the orzo is cooked, about 9 minutes.

Add the spinach and meatballs, and simmer for 2 to 4 minutes, or until the spinach has wilted and the meatballs are well cooked.

Drizzle the remaining 3 tablespoons of oil over the dish and sprinkle with cheese.

# Mushroom cottage cheese stir_fry

serves: 2   **Time:** 20 mins   **Cook Time:** 10 mins

Ingredients

- 1 tablespoon oil (vegetable or olive oil)
- 8 oz mushrooms, sliced
- 1 cup cottage cheese
- 1 small onion, finely chopped
- 2 cloves garlic, minced
- 1 teaspoon ginger, minced
- 1 green chili, finely chopped (optional for heat)
- 1/2 teaspoon cumin seeds
- 1/2 teaspoon turmeric powder
- 1/2 teaspoon garam masala (optional, for added flavor)
- Salt and pepper to taste
- Fresh cilantro or parsley, chopped (for garnish)

Directions

Heat oil in a skillet. Sauté the cumin seeds, garlic, ginger, and optional green chile. Add the mushrooms and simmer until soft. Stir in the cottage cheese and heat through. Sprinkle with turmeric, garam masala (optional), salt, and pepper. Garnish with cilantro or parsley. Serve hot as a side or alongside rice.

Ground Beef and Rice Casserole

serves: 2   **Time: 40 mins**   **Cook Time:** 20 mins

Ingredients

- 1 pound ground beef
- 1 cup uncooked rice
- 1 can (10.5 oz) cream of mushroom soup
- 1 can (10.5 oz) cream of chicken soup
- 1 can (14.5 oz) diced tomatoes, drained
- 1 cup beef broth
- 1 medium onion, diced
- 1 green bell pepper, diced
- 2 cloves garlic, minced
- 1 teaspoon salt
- 1/2 teaspoon black pepper
- 1 teaspoon paprika
- 1 cup shredded cheddar cheese (optional)

Directions

Preheat the oven to 350° Fahrenheit (175° Celsius). Brown one pound of ground beef in a pan and drain the fat. Cook 1 chopped onion, 1 diced green bell pepper, and 2 minced garlic cloves until soft. In a mixing dish, combine the meat and veggies with 1 cup uncooked rice, 1 can each of cream of mushroom and cream of chicken soup, 1 drained can of diced tomatoes, 1 cup beef broth, 1 teaspoon salt, 1/2 teaspoon pepper, and 1 teaspoon paprika. Pour into a greased 9x13-inch casserole dish, cover with foil, and bake for an hour. Optionally, add 1 cup shredded cheddar cheese in the last 10 minutes of baking.
Allow to sit before serving. Enjoy!

Zucchini stir fry

 serves: 2   Time: 20 mins   Cook Time: 15 mins

Ingredients

- 2 medium zucchinis, sliced into thin rounds or half-moons
- 1 tablespoon oil (vegetable or olive oil)
- 2 cloves garlic, minced
- 1 teaspoon ginger, minced
- 1/2 teaspoon red pepper flakes (optional, for heat)
- 1 tablespoon soy sauce
- 1 teaspoon rice vinegar or white vinegar
- Salt and pepper to taste
- Fresh cilantro or green onions, chopped (for garnish)
- Instructions:
- Heat Oil: Heat the oil in a large skillet or frying pan ove

Directions

In a skillet, heat oil over medium-high heat. Sauté minced garlic, ginger, and red pepper flakes until aromatic. Stir in the cut zucchinis and cook until tender-crisp and faintly browned, about 5-7 minutes. Drizzle with soy sauce and vinegar, then season with salt and pepper. Toss to cover evenly. Sprinkle with chopped cilantro or green onions. Serve hot as a side dish or over rice for a quick and satisfying supper.

Lemon Herb Grilled Swordfish

serves: 2   Time: 20 mins   Cook Time: 10 mins

Ingredients

- 1 lb Brussels sprouts, trimmed and halved
- 2 tablespoons olive oil
- Salt and pepper to taste
- 2 tablespoons balsamic vinegar
- 1 tablespoon honey
- 2 cloves garlic, minced
- 2 tablespoons grated Parmesan cheese (optional)

Directions

Grill at a medium-high temperature.
Olive oil, lemon zest, lemon juice, minced garlic, chopped fresh herbs, salt, and pepper should all be combined in a bowl.
After patting the swordfish steaks dry, apply the herb mixture on both sides.
Swordfish steaks should be cooked for 4–5 minutes on each side, or until a fork can easily pierce the flesh.
Take it off the grill and give it some time to rest.
The swordfish steaks should be served with lemon wedges for squeezing over the top.

Pesto Chicken Panini

serves: 2

Time: 15 mins

Cook Time: 6 mins

Ingredients

- 2 boneless, skinless chicken breasts
- Salt and pepper to taste
- 4 tablespoons low-carb pesto (store-bought or homemade)
- 4 slices low-carb bread (look for options with less than 5g net carbs per slice)
- 4 slices mozzarella cheese
- Cooking spray or olive oil for grilling

Directions

Warm up a panini press or grill pan on medium heat.
To taste, add salt and pepper to the chicken breasts.
The chicken breasts should be cooked through and no longer pink in the center after 6 to 8 minutes on each side of the grill.
Take them off the stove and give them some time to rest.
Cut the chicken breasts into thin pieces when they have rested.
Top each slice of bread with 1 tablespoon of low-carb pesto.
Place two slices of bread on top of the cut chicken.
Place a slice of mozzarella cheese on top of the chicken and place the remaining bread slices, pesto side down, on top.
Apply a thin layer of cooking spray or olive oil on the outside of every sandwich.
Arrange the sandwiches on the panini press or grill pan.
Cook the bread for 3–4 minutes on each side, or until the cheese melts and the bread turns golden brown.
Before slicing, remove off the fire and allow them to cool for one minute.
After cutting each sandwich in half diagonally, reheat it.

Cauliflower Fried Rice

serves: 2

Time: 20 mins

Cook Time: 3 mins

Ingredients

- 1 head cauliflower, grated into rice-like texture
- 2 tablespoons olive oil
- 2 cloves garlic, minced
- 1 small onion, diced
- 1 cup mixed vegetables (such as peas, carrots, bell peppers)
- 2 eggs, beaten (optional)
- 2 tablespoons low-sodium soy sauce or tamari
- Salt and pepper to taste

Directions

In a big skillet over medium heat, warm up the olive oil. Cook the onion and garlic until they become tender.
To the pan, add the cauliflower rice and mixed veggies. Sauté the veggies until they are soft.
Spoon beaten eggs into the opposite half of the skillet after pushing the cauliflower mixture to one side. Cook the eggs by scrambling them.
Add the soy sauce and mix everything in the skillet. To taste, add salt and pepper for seasoning. Simmer for a further two to three minutes.
Serve hot as a tasty, low-carb substitute for regular fried rice.

# Stuffed Portobello Mushrooms

serves: 2   Time: 50 mins   Cook Time: 20 mins

Ingredients

- 4 large portobello mushrooms, stems removed
- 1 cup spinach, chopped
- 1/2 cup cherry tomatoes, halved
- 1/4 cup grated Parmesan cheese
- 2 cloves garlic, minced
- 2 tablespoons olive oil
- Salt and pepper to taste
- Fresh parsley for garnish (optional)

Directions

Set oven temperature to 375°F, or 190°C.

On a baking sheet covered with parchment paper, arrange the portobello mushrooms.

Olive oil should be heated in a pan over medium heat. Cook the minced garlic until it becomes aromatic.

Cook the spinach in the pan with chopped leaves until it wilts.

After turning off the heat, add the grated Parmesan cheese and the chopped cherry tomatoes to the pan. Add pepper and salt according to taste.

Fill each portobello mushroom cavity with a spoonful of the spinach mixture.

Pour a small amount of olive oil onto the filled mushrooms.

Bake for 20 to 25 minutes in a preheated oven, or until the filling is cooked through and the mushrooms are soft.

Take out of the oven and sprinkle some fresh parsley on top before serving.

Vegetable Fried Rice

serves: 2   Time: 30 mins   Cook Time: 5 mins

Ingredients

- 2 cups cooked brown rice, chilled
- 2 tablespoons sesame oil
- 2 cloves garlic, minced
- 1 small onion, diced
- 1 cup mixed vegetables (such as peas, carrots, corn)
- 2 green onions, thinly sliced
- 2 tablespoons low-sodium soy sauce or tamari
- 1 tablespoon rice vinegar
- Salt and pepper to taste

Directions

In a large skillet or wok, heat the sesame oil over medium-high heat. Cook the diced onion and minced garlic until they become soft and aromatic.

Cook the mixed veggies in the skillet until they are soft.

Add the cooked rice that has been cooled, stirring to break up any clumps, and heat through.

Pour the beaten eggs into the opposite half of the skillet after pushing the rice mixture to one side. Cook the eggs by scrambling them.

Stir in the rice vinegar, soy sauce, and chopped green onions after combining everything in the skillet. Simmer for a further two to three minutes.

To taste, add salt and pepper for seasoning. Serve hot as a filling and tasty side dish to rice.

SMOOTHIES / DESSERTS

RECIPES

Avocado Berry Smoothie

serves: 2 **Time: 30 mins** **Cook Time:** 10 mins

Ingredients

- 1/2 ripe avocado, peeled and pitted
- 1/2 cup mixed berries (strawberries, raspberries, blueberries)
- 1 cup unsweetened almond milk
- 1 tablespoon chia seeds
- 1/2 teaspoon vanilla extract
- Stevia or erythritol to taste (optional)
- Ice cubes (optional)

Directions

1. Almond milk, chia seeds, avocado, mixed berries, vanilla extract, and sweetener (if used) should all be combined in a blender.
2. Blend till creamy and smooth.
3. If you want your smoothie cooler, add some ice cubes and combine once more.
4. Transfer into glasses and serve right away.

Berry Blast Smoothie

serves: 2 **Time: 30 mins** **Cook Time:** 10 mins

Ingredients

- 1 cup mixed berries (strawberries, blueberries, raspberries)
- 1 ripe banana
- 1/2 cup Greek yogurt (or coconut yogurt for dairy-free)
- 1/2 cup almond milk (or any milk of your choice)
- Optional: 1 tablespoon honey or maple syrup

Directions

1. In a blender, combine almond milk, chia seeds, avocado, mixed berries, vanilla extract, and sweetener (if using).
2. Blend until smooth and creamy.
3. Pour in some ice cubes and blend again if you want your smoothie to be colder.
4. Spoon into glasses and serve immediately.

Mixed Berry Coconut Smoothie

 serves: 2   Time: 30 mins   Cook Time: 10 mins

Ingredients

- 1 cup mixed berries (strawberries, blueberries, raspberries)
- 1/2 cup coconut milk
- 1/2 ripe banana
- 1 tablespoon almond butter
- Ice cubes (optional)

Directions

1. Blend the almond butter, ripe banana, coconut milk, and mixed berries using a blender.
2. Blend till creamy and smooth.
3. If desired, add ice cubes and mix one more.
4. Transfer into glasses and serve right away.

Green Tea Berry Smoothie

 serves: 2   Time: 30 mins   Cook Time: 10 mins

Ingredients

- 1 cup mixed berries (strawberries, blueberries, raspberries)
- 1/2 cup brewed green tea, cooled
- 1/2 cup Greek yogurt (or coconut yogurt for dairy-free)
- Handful of spinach leaves
- Optional: 1 tablespoon honey or maple syrup

Directions

1. Blend together the mixed berries, Greek yogurt, steeped green tea, spinach leaves, and honey or maple syrup, if desired, in a blender.
2. Blend till creamy and smooth.
3. If needed, taste and adjust the sweetness.
4. Transfer into glasses and serve right away.

Cherry Almond Smoothie

serves: 2   Time: 30 mins   Cook Time: 10 mins

Ingredients

- 1 cup frozen cherries
- 1/2 cup almond milk
- 1/4 cup Greek yogurt (or coconut yogurt for dairy-free)
- 1 tablespoon almond butter
- Optional: 1 tablespoon honey or maple syrup

Directions

1. Blend the frozen cherries, Greek yogurt, almond butter, almond milk, and honey or maple syrup, if desired, in a blender.
2. Blend till creamy and smooth.
3. If needed, taste and adjust the sweetness.
4. Transfer into glasses and serve right away.

Strawberry Spinach Smoothie

serves: 2   Time: 30 mins   Cook Time: 10 mins

Ingredients

- 1 cup strawberries, hulled
- Handful of spinach leaves
- 1/2 cup Greek yogurt (or coconut yogurt for dairy-free)
- 1/2 cup almond milk (or any milk of your choice)
- Optional: 1 tablespoon honey or maple syrup

Directions

Blend the strawberries, spinach leaves, Greek yogurt, almond milk, and, if desired, honey or maple syrup in a blender.
Process till creamy and smooth.
If needed, adjust the sweetness by tasting.
After pouring into glasses, serve right away.

 # Decorative Cheese Ball with Crackers

 serves: 2

🕐 **Cook Time:** 2 hours

Ingredients

- 8 oz package of mild cheddar cheese
- 8 oz cream cheese
- 8 oz port wine cheese
- 5 oz pimiento cheese
- 3 tbsp olives with pimiento centers
- 1 ½ cup chopped pecans
- 1 tbsp Worcestershire sauce
- 1 tbsp parsley flakes

Directions

Cheeses such as mild cheddar, cream, port wine, pimiento, Worcestershire sauce, and parsley flakes should all be combined. Blend until well blended.

After forming the dough into a ball, roll it in chopped pecans to coat it well.

Utilize pimiento-centered olives to fashion ornamental designs onto the cheese ball.

Accompany with a few crackers.

Almond Flour Pancakes

 serves: 2

 Time: 30 mins

 Cook Time: 5 mins

Ingredients

- 1/2 cup almond flour
- 2 large eggs
- 1/4 cup unsweetened almond milk (or any milk of your choice)
- 1 tablespoon olive oil or melted butter
- 1 tablespoon erythritol (or any sugar substitute of your choice)
- 1 teaspoon baking powder
- 1/2 teaspoon vanilla extract
- Pinch of salt

Directions

Almond flour, eggs, almond milk, erythritol, baking powder, vanilla extract, and a small amount of salt should all be properly blended and smooth in a mixing bowl before being added to the mixture.

To let the almond flour absorb the liquid and slightly thicken, let the batter sit for five to ten minutes.

Grease a non-stick skillet or griddle with cooking spray or a tiny bit of olive oil and heat it over medium heat.

For each pancake, add 1/4 cup of the batter to the skillet.

Cook the pancakes for two to three minutes on each side, or until the edges seem firm and bubbles begin to appear on the surface.

After flipping the pancakes, fry them for a further one to two minutes on the other side, or until golden.

Serve the almond flour pancakes hot, topped with your favorite pancake toppings.

Black Bean Brownies

 serves: 2   **Time:** 20 mins   **Cook Time:** 35 mins

Ingredients

- 1 can (15 oz) black beans, flushed and depleted
- 3 enormous eggs
- 1/4 cup unsweetened cocoa powder
- 1/4 cup sans sugar, (for example, erythritol or stevia)
- 2 tablespoons coconut oil, softened
- 1 teaspoon vanilla concentrate
- 1/2 teaspoon baking powder
- Spot of salt

Sans sugar chocolate chip

Directions

Set the oven's temperature to 175°C/350°F. Use parchment paper or grease a baking dish.

Black beans, eggs, sugar-free sweetener, cocoa powder, melted coconut oil, vanilla extract, baking powder, and a dash of salt should all be combined in a food processor.

Scrape down the sides as necessary, and blend until creamy and smooth.

Evenly distribute the batter after pouring it into the baking dish that has been ready.

If desired, top with sugar-free chocolate chips.

A toothpick put into the center of the brownies should come out clean after 25 to 30 minutes of baking in a preheated oven.

Before cutting the brownies into squares, let them cool completely.

For a rich, fudgy delight, serve at room temperature.

Bacon, Lettuce, Tomato Dip

serves: 2    **Time: 50 mins**   **Cook Time:** 40 mins

Ingredients

- 1 cup mayonnaise
- 1 cup sour cream
- 1 lb bacon
- ¼ head of lettuce
- 1 medium tomato
- 1 loaf of white bread

Directions

1. Once the bacon is crispy, break it up or cut it into little pieces.
2. Dice the tomato and lettuce into tiny pieces.
3. Mix together mayonnaise, sour cream, cooked bacon, tomato, and lettuce in a mixing dish. Blend well.
4. Serve the dip with crackers or pieces of white bread.

MORE BONUS
RECIPES

Blueberry Quesadilla with Wild Blueberry Sauce

 serves: 2   Time: 30 mins   Cook Time: 20 mins

Ingredients

- One bag (10 oz.) frozen blueberries
- 1/4 Cup sugar
- 1 large Apple
- 1/2 Teaspoon ground cinnamon
- 4 Tbsp. Blueberry fruit spread 4 (8-inch) whole
- wheat tortillas 1 cup (2 oz.) shredded part-skim milk
- Mozzarella cheese 1 cup
- Grated zest of 1 lemon
- 2 Tbsp. dried blueberries
- Ricotta cheeses

Directions

Apple, sugar, cinnamon, and frozen berries should all be combined in a medium pot. Cover, raise to a boil over medium-high heat, then lower the heat and simmer for 10 minutes, or until the fruit is tender. Put away the Wild Blueberry Sauce.

Yields two cups. Each tortilla should have 1 tablespoon of blueberry spread applied to it on the work surface, leaving a 1/2-inch border all around. Mix the ricotta and mozzarella cheese with the zest in a bowl. Each tortilla's half should be covered with 1/2 cup of the cheese mixture. After scattering the mixture with dried blueberries, fold the tortilla over to contain the filling.

Over medium-high heat, preheat a big, heavy skillet or griddle. Cook the quesadillas for three minutes, or until they are crisp and have a light brown bottom.

The leftover sauce remains refrigerated, and covered. For up to five days

Kale Chips

 serves: 2   Time: 40 mins   Cook Time: 20 mins

Ingredients

- 1 bunch of kale, washed and thoroughly dried
- Olive oil spray
- Salt to taste
- Optional seasonings: garlic powder, onion powder, paprika, nutritional yeast

Directions

Preheat your oven to 275°F (135°C).

Remove the stems from the kale leaves and tear the leaves into bite-sized pieces.

Spread the kale pieces in a single layer on a baking sheet lined with parchment paper.

Lightly spray the kale with olive oil and sprinkle with salt and any desired seasonings.

Bake in the preheated oven for 20-25 minutes, or until the kale is crispy but not burnt.

Remove from the oven and let cool before serving.

Coconut Tapioca Pudding

 serves: 2   Time: 30 mins   Cook Time: 20 mins

Ingredients

- 1/2 cup small pearl tapioca
- 2 1/2 cups coconut milk
- 1/3 cup sugar
- 1/2 teaspoon vanilla extract
- Shredded coconut for garnish

Directions

For around half an hour, soak the tapioca pearls in water. After draining, set away.

Heat the coconut milk and sugar in a saucepan over medium heat, stirring to dissolve the sugar.

To the coconut milk that is simmering, add the soaked tapioca pearls. Lower the heat to low and continue cooking, stirring often, until the sauce thickens and the tapioca pearls become transparent about 15 to 20 minutes.

After taking off the heat, whisk in the vanilla essence.

After allowing the pudding to reach room temperature, chill it in the refrigerator for a few hours.

Serve the cooled coconut tapioca pudding with shredded coconut on top.

Seafood Chowder

2-4

35 mints

8

Ingredients:

- 4 cuts bacon slashed
- ¼ medium onion slashed
- 2 medium turnips cut into ½ inch blocks
- 2 ½ cups chicken stock
- ½ teaspoon dried thyme
- ¾ teaspoon salt
- ½ teaspoon pepper
- 1 ½ cups weighty cream
- 1 lb white fish, cut into 1 inch pieces (or 2 jars shellfishes)
- 2 tablespoon spread
- ¾ teaspoon glucomannan

Preparation Steps:

- Cook the bacon in a large saucepan over medium heat until crisp. Using a slotted spoon, remove and drain onto a plate lined with paper towels.
- In the bacon fat, add the onion and turnips and sauté for approximately 5 minutes, or until the onions are soft. After adding the chicken stock, simmer for 10 to 15 minutes, or until the turnip is soft. Add thyme, salt, and pepper for seasoning.
- After adding the fish, boil it for a further four minutes, or until it is cooked through. Add the butter and heavy cream and stir. Stir in the glucomannan toward the end of cooking for a richer broth.
- Top each plate with a few pieces of fried bacon.

Almond Macaroons

serves: 2   Time: 30 mins   Cook Time: 20 mins

Ingredients

- two cups of almond flour
- Half a cup of erythritol (or your preferred sugar alternative)
- Two big egg whites
- A pinch of salt
- 1/4 teaspoon of almond essence

Directions

Set oven temperature to 325°F, or 160°C. Use parchment paper to line a baking sheet.

Combine the erythritol and almond flour in a mixing dish.

Beat the egg whites in another basin with a small teaspoon of salt until stiff peaks form.

Till well blended, gently fold in the beaten egg whites and almond extract into the almond flour mixture.

Drop rounded teaspoons of the mixture, spaced a few inches apart, onto the baking sheet that has been prepared using a spoon or cookie scoop.

Bake for 12 to 15 minutes, or until the edges are golden brown, in a preheated oven.

After a few minutes of cooling on the baking sheet, move the almond macaroons to a wire rack to finish cooling.

Mixed Berries With Coconut Cream

2-4

1 hr 20 mints

8

Ingredients:

- 1 (14-ounce [392 ml]) can full-fat coconut milk
- 1 tablespoon
- (15 ml) maple syrup
- 1 pound (454 g) strawberries, hulled
- 3/4 pound (340 g) blueberries
- 3/4 pound (340 g) raspberries

Preparation Steps:

- Open the can of coconut milk without shaking it, and scoop out the cream sitting at the top of the can (the cream separates from the water when chilled).
- Add the cream to a bowl and stir in maple syrup. Check for sweetness and adjust to taste.

Sweet Potato Bisque Mixed Berries With Coconut CreamCream

8 Servings

cook

1 hr 5 mints

5/10

INGREDIENTS:

- 2 pounds (908 g) orange
- sweet potatoes
- 2 carrots (about 7 ounces [196 g])
- 1 parsnip (about 5 ounces [140 g])
- 1 onion (about 5 ounces [140 g])
- 1 quart + 1 cup (1 L + 235 ml) chicken Bone Broth
- 3/4 cup (180 ml) full-fat coconut milk Sea salt to taste

Preparation Steps:

- Peel and chop the sweet potatoes, carrots, and parsnip. Chop the onion. Add the vegetables and the chicken broth to a stockpot.
- Cover and bring to a boil over high heat, then reduce the heat to medium and cook until the vegetables are tender, about 20 minutes.
- Remove from the heat and blend with an immersion blender until smooth.
- Stir in the coconut milk and season to taste with salt. To assemble: Divide the soup evenly among 5 containers or glass jars.

Carrot Cake Muffins

2   15 mints   6/10

INGREDIENTS:

- 1/3 cup cassava flour
- 1/3 cup tigernut flour
- 2 tablespoons coconut flour
- 1/2 teaspoon ground cinnamon
- 1/2 teaspoon ginger powder
- 1/4 teaspoon baking powder
- Pinch ground cloves
- Pinch sea salt
- 1/4 cup palm shortening
- melted 1/4 cup
- unsweetened applesauce
- 3 tablespoons maple syrup
- 1/2 tablespoon unflavored gelatin powder
- 1/2 cup shredded carrot

Preparation Steps:

- Preheat the oven to 375°F (190°C or gas mark 5) and place the rack in the middle. Line a muffin pan with 5 greaseproof muffin liners.
- In a large bowl, combine the three flours, cinnamon, ginger, baking powder, cloves, and salt.
- In a small bowl, whisk together the palm shortening, applesauce, and maple syrup. Sprinkle the gelatin powder over the mixture, let it bloom for a couple of minutes, then whisk until well blended, ensuring there are no lumps. Mix in the shredded carrots.
- Pour the liquid mixture over the dry ingredients and mix well with a spatula to obtain a smooth batter. Divide the batter evenly among the 5 muffin cups and press down lightly with your fingers. (This prevents air pockets from forming so that the dough holds together better once baked.)
- Bake in the oven until the edges are lightly browned, about 25 minutes, or until a toothpick inserted near the center of a muffin comes out clean. Allow to cool completely on a cooling rack before storing

Strawberry Pâtes De Fruit

5-servings   Cooking   32 mints

Ingredients:

- 1 pound (454 g) strawberries
- 11/3 cups (315 ml) water
- divided
- 3 tablespoons (28 g) gelatin powder
- 11/2 tablespoons (23 ml) maple syrup, or more to taste

Preparation Steps:

- Lightly grease a 9 x 5-inch (23 x 12.7 cm) glass baking dish.
- In a food processor equipped with an S-blade, add the strawberries and 1 cup (235 ml) of the water. Process until smooth, about 30 seconds.
- In a small bowl, combine the remaining 1/3 cup (80 ml) water and gelatin powder. Mix well, making sure all the powder is dissolved and you obtain a gel-like mixture.
- Transfer the strawberry mixture, gelatin, and maple syrup to a saucepan. Warm over medium-low heat for a few minutes, stirring constantly, until all the ingredients are well combined. Do not boil.
- Pour the strawberry mixture into the dish and refrigerate for at least 4 hours, or until firm, preferably overnight.

Conclusion

Throughout this book, you have gained the knowledge and skills needed to elevate your cooking and transform your experience with Mediterranean Diet recipes. From understanding the fundamentals of this diet to mastering the art of incorporating fresh, healthy ingredients, using essential tools, and exploring versatile recipes, you now have a comprehensive guide to making the most of your culinary adventures.

You've learned about Mediterranean Diet recipes, including their versatility, ease of use, and ability to produce consistent, delicious results. Moreover, you have discovered how cooking can become a meditative practice, bringing peace and harmony to your life.

If this book has been helpful to you, please take a moment to leave a review on Amazon. Your feedback is invaluable and helps other readers discover the benefits and joys of embracing Mediterranean Diet recipes. Happy cooking!

ABXTR

NOTES

grocery *list*

produce	meat & fish	frozen

dairy & eggs	baking	deli

canned	beverages	other

grocery *list*

produce	meat & fish	frozen
_____	_____	_____
_____	_____	_____
_____	_____	_____
_____	_____	_____
_____	_____	_____
_____	_____	_____
_____	_____	_____
_____	_____	_____
_____	_____	_____
_____	_____	_____

dairy & eggs	baking	deli
_____	_____	_____
_____	_____	_____
_____	_____	_____
_____	_____	_____
_____	_____	_____

canned	beverages	other
_____	_____	_____
_____	_____	_____
_____	_____	_____
_____	_____	_____

grocery *list*

produce	meat & fish	frozen

dairy & eggs	baking	deli

canned	beverages	other

grocery *list*

produce	meat & fish	frozen
_____	_____	_____
_____	_____	_____
_____	_____	_____
_____	_____	_____
_____	_____	_____
_____	_____	_____
_____	_____	_____
_____	_____	_____
_____	_____	_____
_____	_____	_____

dairy & eggs	baking	deli
_____	_____	_____
_____	_____	_____
_____	_____	_____
_____	_____	_____

canned	beverages	other
_____	_____	_____
_____	_____	_____
_____	_____	_____
_____	_____	_____

meal *planner*

breakfast	lunch	dinner

meal *planner*

breakfast	lunch	dinner

meal *planner*

breakfast	lunch	dinner

Printed in Great Britain
by Amazon